THE MUSE COLONY

THE MUSE COLONY

RUPERT BROOKE, EDWARD THOMAS
ROBERT FROST and FRIENDS

— *DYMOCK~1914* —

KEITH CLARK

REDCLIFFE

First published in 1992 by
Redcliffe Press Ltd
49 Park St, Bristol.

© *Keith Clark*

ISBN 1 872971 30 X

British Cataloguing-in-Publication Data.
A catalogue record for this book is available from the
British Library.

Typeset and printed by
The Longdunn Press Ltd, Bristol.

Contents

Preface

It was while researching an earlier book that I found myself in Dymock with time to spare. In the parish church I was intrigued to discover at the rear of the nave a small display devoted to a group of poets who lived in the parish during the spring and summer of 1914. I came out wanting to know more about how Robert Frost, Lascelles Abercrombie and Wilfrid Gibson had come to be living in this remote corner of North Gloucestershire, attracting to the area writers like Edward Thomas, Rupert Brooke, Eleanor Farjeon, W H Davies and John Drinkwater. So I went the long way home, driving past Gibson's Old Nail Shop and Little Iddens where the Frosts had lived. This book is the result of this chance visit to Dymock.

The story of the Dymock Poets could not have been written without a lot of help from many people and I would like to take this opportunity to thank them, especially Jeff Cooper, Myfanwy Thomas and Michael Gibson. A list of printed sources is given at the end of the book and acknowledgement is due to authors and publishers who have allowed me to quote from their publications or reprint poems under their copyright. My special thanks to the Estate of the author and Jonathan Cape for permission to reproduce the poems by Robert Frost.

Keith Clark

The Dymock Poets

Summer 1914. Britain was in the shadow of a worsening crisis in Europe. War with Germany, for months the subject of speculation, had become a real possibility. Reservists were being called up, the Navy had already been mobilised and the talk in the pubs, shops and parlours all over Britain was of the great 'adventure' to come, a war that, when it happened, was sure to be over in a few months.

In the north-west corner of Gloucestershire, however, in the cottages and farmhouses in and around the village of Dymock, there was another topic of conversation that hot summer of 1914 – the strange people who had begun to move into the area, poets and writers, spies perhaps, it was even suggested.

A group of some of the leading young poets, members of the so-called Georgian movement, had forsaken the literary scene and come to this remote corner of England, and rented picturesque cottages in and around the village of Dymock on the Gloucestershire-Herefordshire border. It was what Helen Thomas, wife of the writer Edward Thomas, described as "a poets' holiday in the shadow of the war."

Liverpool poet Lascelles Abercrombie had been the first to move here, renting The Gallows on the estate of the local landowner, Lord Beauchamp, at Ryton to the south-east of Dymock in 1911 and, although he had already established his reputation, he was to enjoy his richest period in Gloucestershire. He was followed by Wilfrid Gibson, from Northumberland via London, who took a thatched cottage at Greenway Cross to the west of the village. Abercrombie and Gibson persuaded the American poet Robert Frost to leave the suburban countryside in which he was living and discover the 'real' English countryside. He completed what has been called The Dymock Triangle, with the three poets at corners of a triangle with the village of Dymock in the centre. Abercrombie, Gibson and Frost turned this rural corner of England into a haven for the literati of their generation.

Edward Thomas visited Frost three times in the first six months of 1914 before bringing his family down for August, renting rooms in a farmhouse near the cottage rented by the Frosts. The children's writer, Eleanor Farjeon, who was a close friend of the Thomases, also took rooms nearby for a brief holiday. Rupert Brooke and the poet, dramatist and actor John Drinkwater were regular visitors to the Abercrombies and the Gibsons, joining with them in the publication of a quarterly collection of verse, published from Ryton and sent all over the world from the tiny village post office.

The tramp poet, W.H. Davies, stayed with the Gibsons; Arthur Ransome was also a visitor. Edward Marsh, the influential patron of the arts, was attacked by a swarm of wasps when taking a shower at the Abercrombies', drank too much 'mild' beer in the local inns and returned to stay with the Gibsons after Rupert Brooke's untimely death to write his memoir of the young poet. Among Gloucestershire's own literary men, Ivor Gurney, composer and poet, introduced himself to the Abercrombies and kept up a correspondence with them, while John Haines – solicitor, botanist, poet and relative of Catherine Abercrombie – became a close friend of Robert Frost, remaining in touch for decades after the American's return to his native land, through letters and on Frost's few visits back to England. Haines was later to describe the months when Dymock became the centre of contemporary English poetry: ". . . it remains the most beautiful experience in a life which has been more than ordinarily blessed in that way".[1]

This corner of north-west Gloucestershire, so close to the Herefordshire border that Edward Thomas always referred to Leddington as being in the adjacent county, was not an obvious place for such a gathering of poets. It was remote and very rural. It had not always been so, indeed it had a quite surprising history right back to Roman days when it has been speculated it could have been the 'lost' Roman town of Macatonium, and the B4215 road from Dymock to the A4172 at Preston Cross follows the route of a Roman road. In the Middle Ages it is recorded as a town, with a wool trade well enough established (it was from Dymock's flocks that the sheep were selected by Edward III to give to the King of Spain to improve the Spanish sheep breeding stocks) to warrant bringing the costly canal here in the 18th century passing through a 2,170 yard long tunnel between Dymock and Oxenhall. The waterway has long since closed. This was also the fate of the Great Western Railway line between Gloucester and Ledbury, built in 1885 in many places over the course of the now defunct canal. In the days of the Dymock poets, the line was a single track to Gloucester but double to the Herefordshire terminus. It became a single track all along the line in 1917. The line was closed to passengers in 1959 and to goods traffic a few years later.

In the Domesday Book, commissioned only 13 miles away in the city of Gloucester where William The Conqueror held his Christmas 'Witan', or parliament, in 1085, Dymock is shown as one of the most sizeable manors in the county, with 5,652 acres under cultivation and a male population greater than the combined manors of Newent and Kempley. Dymock's early importance is shown in the size and scale of its Norman parish church.

St Mary's is a powerful building that completely dominates the village and large enough to have originally been a Saxon minster. It has many unusual features, including a carved Norman doorway thought to be by a mason of the Dymock School of Sculpture[2] responsible for some exceptional work in nearby churches, including that at Kempley where the frescoes are some of the finest and best preserved in Britain.

The vernacular buildings of Dymock are red brick or black and white timber framed; Ye Olde Cottage and Wood's Cottage are superb examples of cruck-beamed cottages, one of the oldest forms of cottage construction still surviving. Many cottages in the area are still roofed with thatch.

The valley in which Dymock lies is fed by the River Leadon which rises north of Evesbatch in the Malvern Hills near the River Frome and flows south through Bosbury, one of the great manors of Herefordshire, through the picturesque town of Ledbury to Dymock, passing under the road from Greenway Cross to Leddington. It is, as Edward Thomas described, a "narrow country" between the hills of the Cotswolds, the Malverns and between the Severn and Wye rivers. It is a flattish land of shallow valleys and small fields, dominated to the south by the 1,000 ft high May Hill, from the top of which (on a clear day) one can see over 12 counties and some of the most beautiful and spectacular scenery in Britain. On the crown of the dome-shaped hill stands a clump of trees, the subject of many stories and legends; in 'The Everlasting Mercy', John Masefield, born in Ledbury, likens it to a ploughman:

> I've marked the May Hill ploughman stay
> There on his hill, day after day
> Driving his team against the sky . . .

The valley is an extremely lush and fertile landscape, dominated in 1914 by orchards of apples, pears, plums and gages that were greatly prized and graced the top tables of England, as well as fields of soft fruit, strawberries, raspberries, blackcurrants and gooseberries.

In harvest time, Dymock seethed with pickers from as far away as Kent. Huge quantities of the profuse blackberries were sent by rail to a dye factory in the Black Country while sugar beet went to a beet factory in Kidderminster.

The fruit fields took over from the sheep that had been the main form of farming when this area had a thriving woollen industry. In turn, most of the orchards have now been grubbed out, along with many miles of hedgerows, to make way for larger fields of grain crops and for the dairy farming which dominate in Dymock today. Also diminished is the area of woods, once dense with broadleaved trees and firs, and the wildflowers that grew in such profusion.

In spring, the fields, hedgerows and woodland floors became washed in yellow as millions of daffodils growing wild came into flower, a colourful remnant from medieval days when they were cultivated to make dyes.

During the last century and right up to the last war, Dymock daffodils were marketed as blooms in nearby towns, the London flower markets and even by post. What began as a cottage industry became big business employing local women and children and then pickers from outside the area, as John Masefield described in 'Daffodil Fields':

> And there the pickers come, picking for town
>   Those dancing daffodils; all day they pick;
> Hard-featured women, weather-beaten brown,
>   Or swarthy-red, the colour of old brick.

The Great Western Railway ran special trains for the pickers and Easter day-trips to Dymock and other stations along its 'Daffodil Line' from Ledbury to Gloucester. The pickers' trains were on a two-class basis. Very basic carriages with wooden seats served for the itinerant pickers, who included gypsies from the Kent hop-fields, and slightly more comfortable carriages for the day-trippers who travelled not just from the Western towns and cities but also from the capital for a day out amongst the daffodils, many working alongside the 'professional' pickers in much the same way as London's East Enders worked on day trips in the hop fields.

Modern farming methods have taken their toll and today the daffodils no longer flourish in anything like the profusion that the poets saw in 1914. In Kempley and Ryton, however, the wild daffodils, smaller in flower and stem than the garden varieties, still grow in abundance in the woods and forests[3] to give some idea of the glorious sight this must have been.

"I wish I could make you feel what a lovely country this is. When we first came, the meadows were covered with yellow daffodils and the cuckoo had just begun to sing," wrote Robert Frost's wife Elinor to her sister in June 1914. Catherine Abercrombie, Lascelles' wife, described in a radio broadcast how "The sight of the blossoming of the apple and cherry trees in spring was unforgettable, with miles and miles of daffodils pouring over the ground . . ."[4]

Edward Thomas, too, extolled the delights of the Leadon Valley:

In April here I had heard, among apple trees in flower, not the first cuckoo, but the first abundance of day-long calling cuckoos; here the first nightingale's song, though too far off and intermittently, twitched away by gusty night winds; here I found the earliest may blossoms which, by May Day, while I still lingered, began to dapple the hedges thickly and no rain fell yet the land was sweet. . . . Now it was August, and again no rain fell for many days; the harvest was a good one, and after standing long in the sun it was gathered in and put in ricks in the sun, to the contentment of men and rooks. All day the rooks in the wheat-fields were cawing a deep sweet caw, in alternating choirs or all together, almost like sheep bleating, contentedly, on until late evening. The sun shone, always warm, from skies sometimes cloudless, sometimes inscribed with a fine white scatter miles high, sometimes displaying the full pomp of white moving mountains, sometimes almost entirely shrouded in dull sulphurous threats, but vain ones.[5]

Helen Thomas travelled to Dymock to join her husband on the very day in August 1914 that war was proclaimed. She quickly fell under the spell:

The news of the war had of course preceded us, but no excitement disturbed the peace of that beautiful orchard country, with its wealth of choicest apples, pears and plums hanging red and golden and purple from the branches of innumerable fruit trees, which bore in the very truth fruit that were jewels of great price. We, living there with the farmer and his wife, and in the constant society of people who became our intimate and beloved friends, did not then realise all that brooded over our lives. We spent those happy weeks in the open air, in the evenings sitting with our friends and talking – talking of people and life and poetry . . .[6]

Remote though this rural area may have been from anything that could be called a literary tradition, it had remarkably produced a number of people who achieved considerable fame. John Kyrle, born in 1637 at The White House (actually built of red brick) opposite Dymock Church had used his wealth to develop Ross-on-Wye, and achieved literary immortality as 'The Man Of Ross' of Alexander Pope's poem 'Of the Uses of Riches'. This had been written after Pope had discovered during a visit to Ross in 1731 that there was no memorial to Kyrle, who had died seven years earlier:

. . . All our praises why should Lord engross?
Rise honest muse! and sing The Man of Ross:
Pleas'd Vago echoes through her winding bounds
And rapid Severn hoarse applause resounds,
Who hung with woods yon mountains sultry brow?
From the Dry rocks who bid the waters flow?
Not to the skies in useless column lost,
Or in proud falls magnificently lost,
But clear and artless, pouring through the plain,
Health to the sick, and solace to the swain,
Whose causeway parts the vale in shady rows,
Whose seats the weary traveller repose?
Who taught that Heav'n directed spire to rise?
'The Man of Ross' each lisping babe replies . . .

The Poet Laureate John Masefield was born in 1878 in nearby Ledbury in a Victorian red brick and half-timbered house called The Knapp, and was christened at Preston, just a short walk across the fields from where Frost lived in Leddington. Masefield was also closely associated with Pauntley Court, on the other side of Dymock, the birthplace in the 14th century of Richard Whittington, of 'Turn-again-Whittington' fame and which Masefield helped convert into a home for wayfarers by giving fund-raising readings.

Masefield always maintained that as a child he lived in 'Paradise', a sentiment echoed by Elizabeth Barrett Browning. Born near Durham, she moved as a young child to a country house near Ledbury in 1810. Like Masefield and the Dymock poets, she drew upon the local countryside in poems like 'The Last Bower' and 'The Deserted Garden' which was inspired by her home within sight of the Malvern Hills:

> Hills, Vales, Woods, netted in a silver mist,
> Farms, Granges, doubled up among the hills
> And Cattle grazing in the watered vales,
> And Cottage Chimneys smoking from the woods,
> And Cottage Gardens smelling everywhere,
> Confused with smell of orchards.

There were poets, too, of the Dymock poets' own generation living in Gloucestershire, showing their passion for the local landscape in verse. Ivor Gurney (1890–1937) was not only a fine poet but a composer who had studied under Ralph Vaughan Williams and has been called The English Schubert. F.W. Harvey (1888–1957)[7] was born a few miles south of Dymock, but moved at the age of two to Minsterworth, where he is buried. Gurney, a friend of Harvey's from schooldays at King's School in Gloucester visited the Dymock poets, but Harvey did not seek out other literary men. This is to be regretted because, with the backing of influential poets, such as Abercrombie and Thomas, his simple but beautiful verse, often lovingly describing the Gloucestershire countryside, and his exceptional war poetry, might have found the recognition outside the county that it deserves.

Although they did not know each other Harvey's work was certainly known to Abercrombie. On August 17th, 1913, Gurney was able to tell him that their mutual friend, John Haines (1875–1960), in whose solicitor's practice Harvey worked for many years in Gloucester and then Newnham-on-Severn, had reported that Abercrombie thought highly of his work. Ivor Gurney got to know the Abercrombies well and, in later years, Helen Thomas as well.

The Dymock poets were drawn to Gloucestershire by more than a shared love of the countryside or even the need for like-minded companionship at an unsettled time. They were helping spearhead the great change in English poetry. Abercrombie, Gibson and Brooke were amongst the writers who became known as the Georgian Poets, named after an anthology published in

1912 to which they contributed, alongside de la Mare, Masefield, Chesterton, W.H. Davies, and other writers later to become eminent. The anthology was inspired by Edward Marsh, private secretary to Winston Churchill for 23 years and a central and highly influential figure in the cultural, social and political life of the years before, during and to a lesser extent after the First World War.

Marsh did much to further the careers, and the personal lives, of a great many young writers and artists. All the members of the poet fraternity at Dymock had reason to be grateful for knowing Edward Marsh—not just for his 'professional' interest but also for the deep concern he showed towards their welfare.

Georgian Poetry was not a literary movement as such. There was no collectively stated philosophy and in no respect can Marsh's anthology be seen as any kind of literary manifesto. Marsh saw the anthology more as a business venture, a showcase for modern young poets of the new Georgian Age, brought together to widen the audience for contemporary verse. In this the anthology was singularly successful. There was, however, very little cohesion about the selection for the five Georgian Poetry anthologies. Indeed there was a striking diversity. Abercrombie, reviewing the first anthology in *The Manchester Guardian* (January 6th, 1913) wrote:

> . . . it is not easy to find any remarkable community of purpose in this gathering of seventeen contemporary poets. And that is as it should be, if the book really declares the beginning of a new period. There is nothing of a 'school' here, nothing even of a 'movement'.

There was, however, a certain common ground in their work. They were reacting against the high-blown rhetoric and symbolism of the Victorians, the decadence of fin de siècle and the Imperialistic writings of Kipling and others. Their revolt was not a search for new forms, as their critics have been only too keen to point out, but backwards towards an earlier, lyrical tradition. There was a return to common speech, vernacular plainness rather than Victorian grandiloquence. Their verse has a seeming spontaneity, a directness and simplicity of feeling and expression; they believed in writing nothing that they might not say.

There was realism too. The millworker in the heavily industrialised towns and the labourer in the fields were as likely to be the subjects of their poems as the muses of the Greeks had been in the verse of the generation before them. T.S. Eliot was critical of these new-wave poets, writing that "these Georgians caress everything they touch", yet the realism of some of their writings occasionally shocked. The sensibilities of D.H. Lawrence were provoked by the cruelty of certain passages in one poem by Abercrombie, and the directness of Rupert Brooke's 'A Channel Passage' was condemned by many contemporary writers. *The Times Literary Supplement* of August 29th, 1912 thought "His disgusting sonnet on love and sea-sickness ought never to have been printed" although the writer conceded "we are tempted to like him for writing it."

The Georgian poets shared a return to the pastoral tradition; their poetry shows a passion for the English countryside, for its wildlife, its people and their ways.

For most, "back to nature" was restricted to dreams of a romanticised green utopia or occasional escapes from city and garden suburb for picnics and camping weekends. Abercrombie and Gibson, however, took it a step further and moved to the country – Abercrombie once began a poem:

> Here, as I sit beneath my apple trees
> I sing, Now God help all those poor townees!

but thankfully thought better of it – and soon friends and fellow writers were being invited to join them and experience for themselves the delights of the country. These visitors also saw, probably for the first time, the other side to the romanticism of the countryside: the deprivations of the ordinary people in remote villages in a still feudal society. Even Robert Frost, who had seen the poverty of rural dwellings in the USA, was shocked and some years later he described (perhaps with some exaggeration) the life of the peasantry of Dymock to a Californian friend, the poet and book collector Louis Mertins.

> Those English in the hamlets and open country, the genuinely submerged classes, can give you some pointers on destitution, depression, and dejection that are age-lasting. They are used to living on black bread and rancid cheese, mitey cheese. Now and then we would run into one of them in the fields poaching for a hare. We would see the gamekeeper following after, waiting for a chance to nab the poacher and hustle him off to prison. We found that like as not the gamekeeper had his eye on us, squinting out from under his cap. One had to show birth certificate to prove he wasn't a poacher and avoid arrest; and because one didn't have on knee breeches and a red coat they suspected the worst.

> Those poor devils in the country go around with snares to catch rabbits just to get one little taste of meat for their families to take away the infernal smell of rancid cheese or worse out of their nostrils. The authorities were forever invoking the laws of William Rufus and the New Forest – laws that made it safer, as Emerson says, to kill a man than to kill a hare . . .

> . . . In those days we found, still sticking like burrs, the old regard on the part of the common people towards their 'betters'. We came upon the use of the word 'obediance' used for 'obeisance,' which was new to us. The older women, meeting a superior, would bend the knee and made a low bow. They called this (by an understandable evolution) their 'obediance.'

Frost also described the local people as being the "curds and whey population of England – the remnants of the old Saxons". He told Mertins of the cowmen with their two-tined forks, dressed in filthy short-coats, leggings, helmet-hats and with their thin scraggly hair blowing in the wind – these were people who had not changed since the days of *Piers Plowman*, written many centuries before by another poet who had lived within sight of the Malvern Hills.

The cottages into which Abercrombie, Gibson and Frost moved were not holiday homes or the modernised cottages of today's commuters, but real farmworkers' homes, often very basic and lacking the amenities the poets would have taken for granted in the town. In Abercrombie's The Gallows, the 'bathroom', for instance, was merely a curtained-off recess across a courtyard. Frost's Little Iddens had a brick floor and an outside water pump. Perhaps this was all part of the adventure of going 'back to nature'.

The local vicar, the Reverend Gethyn-Jones, author of a history of Dymock, described this grouping of writers as 'The Muse Colony' but there was no original plan to forge a literary community along the lines of, say, Ruskin's agrarian Guild of St George or Eric Gill's religious brotherhood at Ditchling. It was more akin to the colonies set up by expatriates in a foreign country, or the way former 'townies' group together in villages today. As a 'colony' the Dymock Poets lasted only a short period, the war hastening its end, but the effect on all its 'members' was profound, as is reflected in so much of their writing, and life here was almost idyllic despite the international situation.

> It was a lovely land, and we had gotten together with poet friends – English men who were no more a part of the countryside than ourselves – men as little understood by their neighbours as ourselves. With these friends there went on endless talk on high themes, and as we strolled singly, in pairs, or in groups about the hills and valleys to the far Cotswolds and beyond, looking for flowers – botanizing they called it – vasculum in hand, our bonds of friendship tightened.[8]

For a group of impoverished poets in love with the countryside these walks in Gloucestershire, the Cotswolds, the Forest of Dean and Herefordshire, were taken almost daily, certainly in the case of Frost and Thomas and John Haines when he visited Little Iddens. They wandered the woods, lanes, footpaths and hills for a great many miles, enjoying the beauty of a countryside described so fully by Thomas in an article written shortly after his stay in August 1914.

> As we sat on a gate, the elms in a near hedge grew sombre, though clear. Past them rose a field like a low pitched roof dotted over with black stooks of beans and the elms at the top of that rise looked black and ponderous. Those in farther hedges were dimmer and less heavy, some were as puffs of smoke, while just

15

below the long straight ridge of the horizon, a mile or two away, the trees were no more than the shadows of smoke.

Lombardy poplars rose out from the elms, near and far, in twos and threes, in longer or shorter lines, and at one point grouping themselves like the pinnacles of a cathedral. Most farm-houses in the neighbourhood, and even pairs of cottages, possessed a couple or more. If we got astray we could steer by this or that high-perched cluster, in which, perhaps, one tree having lost a branch now on one side, now on the other, resembled a grass stalk with flowers alternating up it. When night came on, any farm-house group might be transmuted out of all knowledge, partly with the aid of its Lombardy poplars. There was also one tree without a house which looked magnificent at that hour. It stood alone, except for a much lesser tree, as it were, kneeling at its feet, on the long swooping curve of a great meadow against the sky; and when the curve and the two trees upon it were clear black under a pale sky and the first stars, they made a kind of naturally melodramatic 'C'est l'empereur' scene such as must be as common as painters in a cypress country.

Whatever road or lane we took, once in every quarter of a mile we came to a farm-house. Only there by the two trees we tasted austere inhuman solitude as a luxury. Yet a man had planted the trees fifty or sixty years back. (Who was it, I wonder, set the fashion or distributed the seedlings?) It was really not less human a scene than that other one I liked at nightfall. Wildly dark clouds broke through the pallid sky above the elms, shadowy elms towering up ten times their diurnal height; and under the trees stood a thatched cottage, sending up a thin blue smoke against the foliage, and casting a faint light out from one square window and open door. It was cheerful and mysterious too. No man of any nation accustomed to houses must have longed for his home at the sight, or suffered for lacking one, or dreamed that this was it.[9]

As well as the walks, there were afternoons and evenings spent reading poetry, in the orchards of Little Iddens, the garden of The Old Nail Shop or around the campfire at The Gallows. There were midnight hunts for ferns by match light under the steep banks of the Leadon and occasional trips to Wales or to Gloucester to visit the cathedral or enjoy the annual Barton Fair.

The poets and their families enjoyed picnics by the Leadon where Frost and his son Carol taught the Abercrombie boys and John Haines how to skip stones on the surface of the water at which, by Haines's account, they were 'prodigious'[10] and how to make javelins out of tree shoots. In the fields near Little Iddens, Thomas taught the Frosts how to play cricket; in the woods near the Gibsons' cottage they all came together for a picnic where Abercrombie sprawled at ease and talked freely while he ate but Gibson, shy and reserved, "acted the host as circumspectly as if he was sitting at a table topped by a damask tablecloth".[11]

There were evenings in each other's cottages, reading poetry, singing folk songs, discussing literature or just gossiping about other poets. There was the

night at Little Iddens when the Abercrombies joined the Frosts, the Thomases
and Eleanor Farjeon and the conversation ranged from a projected Welsh visit
being planned by Abercrombie and Thomas to the exotic Oriental dressing gown
of purple silk that Ezra Pound had worn when he welcomed Frost to London.

And there was the evening at The Old Nail Shop that Gibson described in a
poem to his wife Geraldine:

THE GOLDEN ROOM

Do you remember that still summer evening
When, in the cosy cream washed living room
Of the old Nailshop, we all talked and laughed—
Our neighbours from The Gallows, Catherine
And Lascelles Abercrombie ; Rupert Brooke ;
Eleanor and Robert Frost, living awhile
At Little Iddens, who'd brought over with them
Helen and Edward Thomas ? In the lamplight
We talked and laughed ; but, for the most part, listened
While Robert Frost kept on and on and on,
In his slow New England fashion, for our delight,
Holding us with shrewd turns and racy quips,
And the rare twinkle of his grave blue eyes ?

We sat there in the lamplight, while the day
Died from rose-latticed casements, and the plovers
Called over the low meadows, till the owls
Answered them from the elms, we sat and talked—

Now, a quick flash from Abercrombie, now,
A murmured dry half-heard aside from Thomas ;
Now, a clear laughing word from Brooke ; and then
Again Frost's rich and ripe philosophy,
That had the body and tang of good draught cider
And poured as clear a stream.

                           'Twas in July
On nineteen fourteen that we talked
Then August brought the war, and scattered us.

Now, on the crest of an Aegean isle,
Brooke sleeps, and dreams of England : Thomas lies
'Neath Vimy Ridge, where he, among his fellows,
Died, just as life had touched his lips to a song.

And nigh as ruthlessly has life divided
Us who survive ; for Abercrombie toils
In a Black Northern town, beneath the glower
Of hanging smoke ; and in America

Frost farms once more ; and, far from the old Nailshop,
We sojourn by the Western Sea.

And yet,
Was it for nothing that the little room,
All golden in the lamplight, thrilled with golden
Laughter from the hearts of friends that summer night ?
Darkness has fallen on it ; and the shadow
May never more be lifted from the hearts
That went through those black years of war, and live.

And still, wherever men and women gather
For talk and laughter on a summer night,
Shall not that lamp rekindle ; and the room
Glow once again alive with light and laughter ;
And, like a singing star in Time's abyss,
Burn golden-hearted through oblivion?

On another evening all the poets were invited to what proved to be a bibulous dinner at the farmhouse where Eleanor Farjeon was staying. They all seem to have acquired quite a taste for native cider and perry and even Frost, who had come to Little Iddens a teetotaller, fell under its spell. In those days it was common for farms to grow their own cider apples and perry pears, wash, pulp and press them and ferment the juice. Cider and perry formed more than just a social drink, it was part of the farm worker's wages; at harvest time it was essential for a farmer to have a barrel and some cheese for his workforce of mostly casual labour. The orchards of cider apples, much more bitter than normal eating apples or cookers, are still prevalent, though much diminished in number since the poets' time, despite mass production at Much Marcle and Hereford. Perry production has all but disappeared in this area today.

These literary young people were not an insular group. They mixed freely with the local people in the lanes, local shops, in the pubs, in the fields when they were allowed to help pick the precious fruit. They made friends with many of the local children, too.

"We first met up with the six poets who took long walks & came to meet us at Little Marcle School as we came out at 3.45," wrote 80-year old Mrs Ellen Neale to the vicar of Dymock, the Reverend Legg in 1982.[12] Mrs Neale was eleven years old when she and her two sisters used to meet the poets after school in 1914. At that time she lived in Preston, which was reached by footpath from Leddington:

They would walk home with us & play marbles, skipping & Hop Scotch & hoop bowling according to the season of games we played, often when we got to Preston Cross as it was then with 4 ponds on either side & huge oak and elm

18

trees, poplars & ash trees—we would all flop down & sit under the biggest oak tree I've ever known, in its shade, & talk about the beauty everywhere around us and ask us what we had learnt on our weekly nature rambles at school. They taught us the names of plants & flowers which we didn't know & which grew in their part of the world or country. On looking back I think we must have appeared to older folk like the Pied Piper of Hamelin following them. They asked us where they could buy milk & butter at a farm so we told them to go to Parkfield Farm where Mr & Mrs Allen farmed & who got to know them all & supplied them with milk & butter & gave them cake & a glass of Buttermilke each week when she was churning.

After their rest under the huge oak tree, the children and the adults parted; the children to their home and the poets to theirs.

There were times when the poets did not welcome each other's company. Sometimes Mrs Gibson would not let Thomas and Frost into The Old Nail Shop when her husband was working on a poem. This was ridiculed a little by the two writers, but behind their scorn, according to Helen Thomas,[13] lay a certain honest jealousy: Gibson was at this time better known and better paid than they were and his work eagerly accepted by American magazines. As a group however they got on well despite these petty jealousies – and Thomas's honesty in his reviews of the others' work which, in their eyes, must have seemed a little harsh:

> Wilfrid Wilson Gibson long ago swamped his small delightful gift by his abundance. He is essentially a minor poet in the bad sense, for he is continually treating subjects poetically, writing about things instead of creating them.[14]

In fact, Thomas thought highly of both Gibson and Abercrombie, the latter's work in particular he lavishly praised as well as criticised.

Thomas and Frost became close friends, cementing in Dymock a profound friendship that began in London earlier in 1914. For Edward Thomas it saw the turning point in his life, for during their walks around Leddington, the evenings spent in Little Iddens or with their families in the neighbouring fields and orchards, Frost persuaded the critic that his true path lay as a poet. Frost had so much in common, intellectually and emotionally, with Thomas that he later stated he could not at that time envisage being without him, and had tried to persuade Thomas to join him in America. Frost also benefitted from his Dymock friendships since Gibson, Abercrombie and especially Thomas were instrumental in helping the American become established as a major poet, not just in this country but also in his native land.

It was not all talk, fun and country walks; there were poems and articles to write, anthologies to compile and the quarterly periodical *New Numbers* to be put together and sent to subscribers. The countryside, the woods, the daffodils and the thatched cottages were to inspire all the poets, especially Gibson and Abercrombie, whose love of the area permeates their writings. Gibson wrote lyrically of his thatched cottage at Greenway Cross, of the starlings nestling in the roof in 'The Old Nail Shop', of its 'black timbers and old rosy brick' in the poem 'Home', of the July evening in 1914 when the Muse Colony congregated in 'The Golden Room' and how he found his 'own hearthstone' in the former nail maker's cottage:

SO LONG HAD I TRAVELLED THE LONELY ROAD

So long had I travelled the lonely road,
Though now and again a wayfaring friend
Walked shoulder to shoulder and lightened the load,
I often would think to myself as I strode –
No comrade will journey with you to the end.

And it seemed to me, as the days went past
And I gossiped with cronies or brooded alone
By wayfaring fires, that my fortune was cast
To sojourn by other men's hearths to the last
And never to come to my own hearthstone.

The lonely road no longer I roam:
We met, and were one in the heart's desire:
Together we came through the wintry gloam
To the little old house by the Greenway home
And crossed the threshold and kindled the fire.

For Abercrombie, the fir trees behind his home at Ryton provided the inspiration for a lengthy poem, called 'Ryton Firs' and dedicated to his sons. It begins with the felling of firs to make pit props for the Welsh mines and ends with a jubilant romp through the countryside beneath the Malvern Hills, with the almost inevitable reference to the fields of daffodils:

It is known to the world what a sight may be seen
In Herefordshire and Glostershire
As soon as earth remembers how to flower;
In a flood running over the fresh of the green
The daffodils pour like a cool fire . . .

So frequently do the daffodils feature in the verse of the poets associated with this area that there is little wonder that Paul Claudel of the French Embassy in Japan should have criticised contemporary British poetry to the poet Robert Nichols in 1923: "I cannot like your daffodeel poetry – there is too much daffodeel round your English Helicon!"[15]

20

NOTES

1 John Haines, *Gloucester Journal*, December 1941.
2 See Eric Gethyn-Jones, *The Dymock School of Sculpture*, (Phillimore & Co, 1979).
3 The Windcross Public Paths project marked out a Daffodil Way around Dymock in 1988. An eight mile circular walk, backed by a printed guide, was signposted with yellow arrowheads.
4 Catherine Abercrombie, 'Memoirs of a Poet's Wife', *The Listener*, November 15th, 1956.
5 Edward Thomas, 'This England', *The Nation*, November 7th, 1914.
6 Helen Thomas, *World Without End*. First published 1931, later reprinted with *As It Was*, (Heinemann, 1935).
7 Frances Townsend, *The Laureate of Gloucestershire. The Life and Work of F.W. Harvey, 1888–1957*, (Redcliffe Press Ltd, 1988).
8 Catherine Abercrombie, ibid.
9 Edward Thomas, ibid.
10 Louis Mertins, *Robert Frost: Life and Talks-Walking*, (University of Oklahoma Press, 1965).
11 Eleanor Farjeon, *Edward Thomas: The Last Four Years*, (Oxford University Press, 1979).
12 Letter is to be seen in the Dymock Poets display in Dymock Church.
13 Helen Thomas, *Time & Again: Memoirs & Letters*, (Carcanet Press, 1978).
14 Review by Edward Thomas in *The Daily Chronicle*, May 18th, 1908.
15 Paul Claudel to the poet Robert Nichols, 1923, retold by the latter to Edward Marsh.

Lascelles Abercrombie

Lascelles Abercrombie was the first to move to Gloucestershire. His older sister had married a gentleman farmer and in 1910 she settled in Much Marcle, across the border in Herefordshire a few miles from Dymock. It was here that Abercrombie first came before moving to The Gallows at Ryton, to the south east of Dymock. His sister had first noticed The Gallows, a pair of cottages on Lord Beauchamp's estate that had been heavily renovated for one of his land agents. When the employee moved elsewhere, the cottages fell empty and Lord Beauchamp was persuaded to rent it to Abercrombie and his family.

The Gallows stood high above the lane, shrouded by elm-trees and flanked by a cherry orchard and close to the Redmarley Hills which at that time were densely covered with larch woods. The garden, yellow with evening primroses and mullein, was, says John Haines, "one of the most beautiful I ever saw".[1]

The house is no more, having been allowed to fall into disrepair and then demolished, as Frost, who stayed here in the winter of 1914, recounted in a verse of his later poem 'The Thatch':

> They tell me the cottage where we dwelt
> Its wind-torn thatch goes now unmended
> Its life of hundreds of years has ended
> By letting the rain I knew outdoors
> In on the upper chamber floors.

The joined cottages were reached from the road by steep stone steps. The older and smaller of the two was typical of the area, half-timbered and whitewashed plaster over red brick walls. Its thatched roof, so steeply pitched that the eaves were shoulder high, was thatched with wheat straw over old rye. This older cottage was known as The Study because it was here that Abercrombie wrote in the main downstairs room; he and Catherine had their bedroom upstairs as did the children. A passageway linked The Study with the larger, red sandstone cottage, to which an annexe had been added to accommodate a kitchen, pantry and a shed, and there were three upstairs bedrooms. It was here that Frost and his family stayed when they first came to Dymock and in mid-September, 1914, when they vacated Little Iddens. The house lacked electricity, running water, mains drainage and much else but nonetheless charmed all its visitors. Edward Marsh after his first visit to The Gallows (on August 17th, 1913, at a time when Gibson, too, was planning to move to Dymock) wrote to Rupert Brooke:

. . . it's the most delicious little house, black and white, with a stone courtyard, and crimson ramblers, and low-beamed ceilings . . . The bathroom is a shed out of doors, with a curtain instead of a door, a saucer bath which you fill by means of an invention of Lascelles' (who was a scientist before he was a poet) a long tube of red india rubber, with a funnel at the end, which you hang on a pump on the other side of the path – cold water alas![2]

Brooke later visited The Gallows himself and also fell for its charms, writing to Russell Loines in 1914:

Abercrombie's is the most beautiful you can imagine; black-beamed & rose-covered. And a porch where one drinks great mugs of cider, & looks at fields of poppies in the corn. A life that makes London a foolish affair.

As well as charm, The Gallows had an interesting history. Many centuries earlier a man living at the Harrow called Jock of Dymock had the habit of lurking at night in one of the animal tunnels near the church. With antlers fixed to his shoulders he would rush out of the tunnel and scare passers-by. He met a sad end – he was caught at Ryton poaching the king's deer and was hanged on the spot, on the site where The Gallows was later built.

At Ryton, Lascelles and Catherine Abercrombie enjoyed what seems an idyllic life of writing and reviewing in the morning and walking the countryside of Lord Beauchamp's estate in the afternoon. It was certainly a way of living that must have seemed strange and Bohemian to the local people. They had a gypsy tent permanently pitched in the garden under the elms that they called The Seven Sisters, where on fine evenings they would cook their meals in an iron pot over an open fire. Often their friends would join them and, after discussing the next issue of their periodical *New Numbers*, Drinkwater, Gibson and Brooke sat with the Abercrombies by the light of the fire and read aloud their latest poems to each other while Catherine Abercrombie "lay on a stoop of hay and listened and watched the stars wander through the elms and thought I really had found the why and wherefore of life."[3]

Life for Lascelles Abercrombie had begun in 1881, at Ashton-under-Mersey. He was the eighth of nine children of stockbroker William Abercrombie and Sarah Ann. Educated at private schools he read Greek and Latin from 1900 to 1902, at a college only a few miles north of Dymock, and then science at Owen College, Manchester. As a young boy he had shown an unusual devotion to the arts, though on leaving college he became a trainee quantity surveyor before turning to journalism as a book reviewer for the *Liverpool Courier*, writing poetry in his spare time. After some of his verses had appeared in magazines, he produced his first book, *Interlude and Poems* in 1908, which was well received by the critics.

Having first arranged to continue reviewing for *The Courier* and other Liverpool papers, as well as for the *Manchester Guardian*, Abercrombie moved to Gloucestershire, to Much Marcle, where he published *Mary and the Bramble*, and then to Ryton, a hamlet between Dymock and Redmarley D'Abitot, where the lane from Dymock meets that from Bromsberrow Heath to Ketford, and where the River Leadon passes under the lane on its way to the Severn.

> Here I am in a cottage in Gloucestershire, living the life (or very nearly) I have always wanted to live! – How did that happen? I scarcely know. I have seen a man score a try in a football match: out of the midst of a long confused struggle, in which he and his side seemed hopelessly pressed right up against their own goal, he suddenly got the ball and saw this opening; and away down the whole length of the field he raced, and none to stop him. So it must have been with me: the opening came, and without stopping to think, I broke away and ran.[4]

While his reputation as a critic and a poet grew, times were not always easy and by 1914, when the Abercrombies were expecting their third child, the financial situation had become serious enough to cause consternation among their friends.

When his reviews for the *Manchester Guardian* came to an end, Catherine Abercrombie even suggested that he went 'harvesting' – but he was not really strong enough to contemplate such exhausting labour. His friends, through Gibson, rallied around: Walter de la Mare and Edward Thomas put him in touch with a relief fund set up to help struggling men of letters, and Edward Marsh, Gosse and the Poet Laureate, Robert Bridges, lent their support. Abercrombie's situation was eased though, like Thomas, he was forced to write reviews and articles for income at the expense of his poetry. In the same year, Abercrombie calculated his earnings for Marsh: in the four years 1909 to 1913 his earnings had been between £210 and £220 a year, about £4 a week.

Despite his financial problems, Abercrombie revelled in the country life, in the peace and tranquillity and the degree of freedom it gave him.

> Now I could do what I liked. Or very nearly. At any rate now when I had finished writing for the night I could step out of doors and smell country air and hear the stream sounding and the owls calling. What great things I meant to do, now I was my own man and living at last in the country! – yes and to crown all, living in that country which is the best part of the most English part of England! How full I was of the things I wanted to do![5]

His love of his new home is nowhere better illustrated than in 'Ryton Firs', the poem about the larch woods to the rear of The Gallows, and dedicated to his three sons, David, Michael and Ralph, all born at Ryton.

Lascelles Abercrombie

RYTON FIRS

FOR DAVID, MICHAEL, RALPH

Dear boys, they've killed our woods: the ground
Now looks ashamed, to be shorn so bare;
Naked lank ridge and brooding mound
Seem shivering cowed in the April air.

They well may starve, hills that have been
So richly and so sturdily fleeced!
Who made this upland, once so green,
Crouch comfortless, like an ill-used beast?

There was a fool who had pulled fierce faces
At his photographer thirty years;
He swore, Now I'll put you through your paces,
Jaegers, Uhlans, and Grenadiers!

Was he to blame? Or the looking-glass
That taught him his moustachioes?
How could that joke for an Attila pass?
Who was to blame? Nobody knows.

He but let loose the frantic mood
That toppled Europe down pell-mell;
It rippled against our quietude,
And Ryton Firs, like Europe, fell.

Now the axe hews, the bill-hook lops.
The owls have flown to Clifford's Mesne,
The foxes found another copse;
The badger trotted to Mitcheldean.

But where is our cool pine-fragrance fled?
Where now our sun-fleckt loitering hours,
Wading in yellow or azure or red,
Daffodil, bluebell, foxglove flowers?

Where is our spring's woodland delight
To scatter her small green fires like dew?
Our riding, a blade of golden light
Cleaving our summer shade in two?

The wind comes noiseless down the hill
That once might just have left the sea,
And would our Glostershire windows fill
With a sound like the shores of Anglesey.

25

The poor trees, all undignified,
Mere logs, that could so sing and gleam,
Laid out in long rows side by side
Across the sloping ground, might seem

A monstrous march of rugged brown
Caterpillars, gigantically
Over the hill-top swarming down
To browse their own lopt greenery.

The last we saw of our lovely friends!
Cannibal grubs! – Then came the wains
To cart them off; their story ends
Not upright still in the winds and the rains

(As tall trees hope to end) at sea,
In graces drest that whiter shine
Then glittering winter: no, but to be
Props in a Glamorgan mine.

So come: where once we loved their shade,
We'll take their ghost an offering now.
Here is an image I have made:
Guarini and Tasso showed me how.

.   .   .   .   .

Ryton Firs are alive again! And I
In the heart of them am happy once again!

All round the knoll, on days of quietest air,
Secrets are being told: if it were high wind,
And the talk of the trees as loud as roaring drums,
Still 't would be secrets, shouted instead of whisper'd.

There must have been a warning given once:
'No tree, on pain of withering and sawfly,
To reach the slimmest of his snaky toes
Into this mounded sward and rumple it;
All trees stand back: taboo is on this soil.' –

The trees have always scrupulously obeyed.
The grass, that elsewhere grows as best it may
Under the larches, countable long nesh blades,
Here in clear sky pads the ground thick and close
As wool upon a Southdown wether's back;
And as in Southdown wool, your hand must sink
Up to the wrist before it finds the roots.
A bed for summer afternoons, this grass;
But in the spring, not too softly entangling
For lively feet to dance on, when the green

26

Flashes with daffodils. From Marcle way,
From Dymock, Kempley, Newent, Bromesberrow,
Redmarley, all the meadowland daffodils seem
Running in golden tides to Ryton Firs,
To make the knot of steep little wooded hills
Their brightest show: O bella età de l'oro!
Now I breathe you again, my woods of Ryton:
Not only golden with your daffodil light
Lying in pools on the loose dusky ground
Beneath the larches, tumbling in broad rivers
Down sloping grass under the cherry trees
And birches: but among your branches clinging
A mist of that Ferrara-gold I first
Loved in those easy hours you made so green.
And hark! you are full of voices now! as if
Ferrara day-dreams had come back to earth
In Glostershire, transforming to a troop
Of lads and lasses, and presently a dance,
Those mornings when your alleys of long light
And your brown rosin-scented shadows were
Enchanted with the laughter of my boys.

THE VOICES
'Follow my heart, my dancing feet,
Dance as blithe as my heart can beat:
Dancing alone can understand
What a heavenly way we pass,
Treading the green and golden land,
Daffodillies and grass.'

'I had a song, too, on my road,
But mine was in my eyes;
For Malvern Hills were with me all the way,
Singing loveliest visible melodies
Blue as a south-sea bay;
And ruddy as wine of France
Breadths of new-turn'd ploughland under them glowed.
'Twas my heart then must dance
To dwell in my delight;
No need to sing when all in song my sight
Moved over hills so musically made
And with such colour played. –
And only yesterday it was I saw
Veil'd in streamers of grey wavering smoke
My shapely Malvern Hills.
That was the last hail-storm to trouble spring:
He came in gloomy haste,
Pusht in front of the white clouds quietly basking,

27

In such a hurry he tript against the hills,
And stumbling forward spilt over his shoulders
All his black baggage held,
Streaking downpour of hail.
Then fled dismayed, and the sun in golden glee
And the high white clouds laught down his dusky ghost.'

'For all that's left of winter
Is moisture in the ground.
When I came down the valley last, the sun
Just thawed the grass and made me gentle turf;
But still the frost was bony underneath.
Now moles take burrowing jaunts abroad, and ply
Their shovelling hands in earth
As nimbly as the strokes
Of a swimmer in a long dive under water.
The meadows in the sun are twice as green
For all the scatter of fresh red mounded earth,
The mischief of the moles:
No dullish red, Glostershire earth new-delved
In April! And I think shows fairest where
These rummaging small rogues have been at work.
If you will look the way the sunlight slants
Making the grass one great green gem of light,
Bright earth, crimson and even
Scarlet, everywhere tracks
The rambling underground affairs of moles:
Though 'tis but kestrel-bay,
Looking against the sun.'

'But here's the happiest light can lie on ground,
Grass sloping under trees
Alive with yellow shine of daffodils!
If quicksilver were gold,
And troubled pools of it shaking in the sun,
It were not such a fancy of bickering gleam
As Ryton daffodils when the air but stirs.
And all the miles and miles of meadowland
The spring makes golden ways,
Lead here; for here the gold
Grows brightest for our eyes,
And for our hearts lovelier even than love.
So here, each spring, our daffodil festival.'

'How smooth and quick the year
Spins me the seasons round!
How many days have slid across my mind
Since we had snow pitying the frozen ground!

Then winter sunshine cheered
The bitter skies; the snow,
Reluctantly obeying lofty winds,
Drew off in shining clouds,
Wishing it still might love
With its white mercy the cold earth beneath.
But when the beautiful ground
Lights upward all the air,
Noon thaws the frozen eaves,
And makes the rime on post and paling steam
Silvery blue smoke in the golden day.
And soon from loaded trees in noiseless woods
The snows slip thudding down,
Scattering in their trail
Bright icy sparkles through the glittering air;
And the fir-branches, patiently bent so long,
Sigh as they lift themselves to rights again.
Then warm moist hours steal in,
Such as can draw the year's
First fragrance from the sap of cherry wood
Or from the leaves of budless violets;
And travellers in lanes
Catch the hot tawny smell
Reynard's damp fur left as he sneakt marauding
Across from gap to gap;
And in the larch woods on the highest boughs
The long-eared owls like grey cats sitting still
Peer down to quizz the passengers below.'

'Light has killed the winter and all dark dreams.
Now winds live all in light,
Light has come down to earth and blossoms here,
And we have golden minds.
From out the long shade of a road high-bankt,
I came on shelving fields;
And from my feet cascading,
Streaming down the land,
Flickering lavish of daffodils flowed and fell;
Like sunlight on a water thrill'd with haste,
Such clear pale quivering flame,
But a flame even more marvellously yellow.
And all the way to Ryton here I walkt
Ankle-deep in light.
It was as if the world had just begun;
And in a mind new-made
Of shadowless delight
My spirit drank my flashing senses in,

29

And gloried to be made
Of young mortality.
No darker joy than this
Golden amazement now
Shall dare intrude into our dazzling lives:
Stain were it now to know
Mists of sweet warmth and deep delicious colour,
Those lovable accomplices that come
Befriending languid hours.'

THE DANCE

    It is known to the world what a sight may be seen
    In Herefordshire and Glostershire
As soon as earth remembers how to flower;
    In a flood running over the fresh of the green
    The daffodils pour like a cool fire:
Keep off and mind your manners, you young man.
    It is like as the morning were spread on the ground
    In Herefordshire and Glostershire,
And we were dancing on the golden hour;
    Such a shimmering gleam is on meadow and mound,
    And giving our minds such bright attire:
Leave eyeing me so bold, you forward maid.

    We will call for a sorrow to pester her, she
    Who's robbing us for the market-buyer,
The crone who strips the field our dances scour;
    And especially everyone spoiling our glee
    With trouble of love and love's desire:
Keep off and mind your manners, you young man.

    And a sorrow the farmer shall have for his spite
    Who scythes at our gold before it tire,
Because the blue leaves make his mown grass sour;
    And another who brings on our shining delight
    The tarnishing moods sweethearts require:
Leave eyeing me so bold, you forward maid.

In Gloucestershire Abercrombie enjoyed his richest period as a poet. In the year he moved to Ryton he wrote the work which brought him to the attention of the critics and the poetry-reading public. 'The Sale of St Thomas' is a lengthy prose poem, of some 500 lines, dedicated to Arthur Ransome and vividly tells of St Thomas's doubts as he sat upon the quay facing the sea voyage to India, listening to the horrendous tales of the captain, to whom he is sold by the Stranger who claims him to be his runaway servant. The critics greeted the work, which he published himself from Ryton, with enthusiasm. *The Nation* (March 8th, 1913) declared: "Mr Abercrombie as a poet has an astonishing power of dramatic psychological analysis. He is a vehement, imaginative thinker . . . The vigour and distinction of his phrases is a continual delight." *The Times Literary Supplement* of February 27th, 1913 contained a similarly extravagant review: "Of all the poetic talents which have appeared since the beginnings of the century, his is the most conspicuous vision of breadth and intensity." Walter de la Mare in an article in *The Edinburgh Review*, April 1913, was even more enthusiastic: "The verse blazes with radiance, jets, leaps, dims, insinuates with every turn and twist of the narrative."

Edward Thomas reviewed Abercrombie's verse favourably, and with his usual erudition and discrimination. His honesty as a reviewer brought him into some conflict with Catherine Abercrombie; as he told Gordon Bottomley in a letter dated December 1914: ". . . Mrs Abercrombie is a little hostile because I sometimes criticise Lascelles." It was aspects of his work he criticised, not his talent or personal qualities. After meeting Abercrombie for the first time at Ryton in May 1914, Thomas again wrote to Bottomley that he liked Abercrombie and expressed concern about his health. Catherine Abercrombie's hostility towards Thomas was similarly not personal – she wrote of him many years later:

> I think Edward was the most beautiful person I have ever seen. It was quite a shock on first meeting him, unless one had been warned. He suffered very much from recurring melancholy, which stamped itself on his face but only made his beauty more apparent.[6]

For all the critics' praise, Abercrombie's success did not last; today his verse seems turgid and wordy, his themes too metaphysical and heavy and his work is included only in a few anthologies while his contemporaries, notably Brooke, Thomas, Frost, de la Mare and W.H. Davies became some of the best known poets of their generation. The extravagant praise of Abercrombie's work was not universal. D.H. Lawrence, on the publication of 'The End of the World' in the second volume of *New Numbers*, wrote to Edward Marsh: "I hate and detest his ridiculous yokels and all the silly hash of his bucolics; I loathe his rather nasty efforts at cruelty . . . what is wrong with the man? – there's something wrong with his soul. 'Mary and The Bramble' and 'Sale of St Thomas' weren't like this. They had a certain beauty of soul, a certain highness which loved . . . I wish to heaven he were writing the best poems that ever were written, and there he turns out this." (Lawrence and Abercrombie had met the year before in Italy and Lawrence then wrote to Marsh: "Abercrombie *is* sharp – he is much more intellectual than I imagined: keener, more sharp-minded. I shall enjoy talking to him.")[7]

Ezra Pound was not an admirer of Abercrombie's. At some time Abercrombie had written that poetry would benefit from a return to Wordsworth as a source of inspiration. Pound disagreed violently and excessively, writing to Abercrombie: "Stupidity carried beyond a certain point becomes a public menace. I hereby challenge you to a duel, to be fought at the earliest moment that is suited to your convenience." Using his prerogative as the challenged party to choose the weapon, Abercrombie suggested that they bombard each other with unsold copies of their own books – a witty response that caused Pound to call off his challenge. Perhaps, it has been suggested, he was worried that he might be embarrassed by finding his own arms full and his opponent weaponless.

Robert Trevelyan was the first visitor to The Gallows and he invited the family back to stay with him in the villa he rented near Florence and which had become something of a haven for British writers. This was where Abercrombie first met Lawrence, who was then living in a fisherman's cottage at Fiascherino.

The young Gloucester poet, Ivor Gurney, turned up at The Gallows unexpectedly and was welcomed by Catherine Abercrombie:

> I was playing with my little boys in a field near our cottage one day when a youth in khaki came walking towards us, asking if I could direct him to Lascelles Abercrombie's cottage, as he wanted to see it, and him, if possible. I took him home to tea and we became friends, but he had to return to the Front. I used to write and send him literary papers, but after a time we lost touch with him and found he had been put into an asylum as his mind had been greatly affected, and there he wrote beautiful verse often spoilt by incoherences but showing what a good poet he might have been."[8]

John Haines was a regular visitor:

> "I often think of my first visit to the cottage with its yard thick thatch, reaching, as I imagine it, almost to the ground, and Abercrombie and John Drinkwater talking ecstatically on Poetic Drama, in that enchanted garden, with a cherry orchard close by; the garden itself, as I seem to see it, a mass of tall, yellow, evening primroses, and equally tall and equally yellow mulleins; and cider being consumed from fat, round, yellow mugs . . ."[9]

On that first visit there was a night-time adventure after they heard the cry of a trapped rabbit somewhere "in those slightly uncanny woods". Abercrombie and his guests carried out a frenzied but unsuccessful search: ". . . tearing our way through brake and bramble, ever the cry failing us as we neared it."

> On other days there were gorgeous sunlit walks over the hills behind the cottage to Redmarley, or by the vale to Wilfrid Gibson, close by at The Greenway, or to Robert Frost, the American poet, two miles away at Ledington, or best of all, down between the hedges to Ketford Bridge, and over the top by the farm, and along the wonderfully flowery valley of the Leadon itself to Payford Bridge; and daffodils, daffodils everywhere, on Callow Farm to one side, and in the woods on the other, and, when the daffodils were over, other flowers like the Star of Bethlehem, the delicate Spreading Bell-flower and the dark blue Sage . . .[10]

Edward Marsh was a welcomed visitor to The Gallows. His manner endeared him to Catherine Abercrombie on his first visit – "one felt he had the same huge respect for each person he met whatever their walk in life"[11] – and she appreciated the way he made no sign of noticing the basic nature of their home and behaved just as he would have done at a stately home. During his stay he was attacked by a swarm of wasps in the bathroom, but would not leave the room until he had got his monocle fixed firmly in his eye and could find his clothes. Marsh was obviously as taken with Catherine Abercrombie as she was with him:

> "Mrs Abercrombie is a delightful woman, *batie sur les grandes lignes*, rather βοῶπις, rather Madonna, not exactly beautiful, but very fresh, and very reassuring, extremely humorous and intelligent, perfect wife-and-mother. I've spent most of this morning with her cutting up French beans and peeling potatoes, I love domestic occupations. There are 2 charming little boys, David aged 3, and Michael, who is very beautiful, about one. Michael is the charmer – he sits in a pen in the dining room, made of wooden rails, with an abacus let into the side, and full of stuffed animals."[12]

While at The Gallows, Marsh explored the local countryside and he and his host climbed May Hill "from which we should have seen all the Kingdoms of the earth, but for a thick haze" and they visited many of the local inns on the way where Abercrombie persuaded Marsh to 'swill' mild beer. In the evenings there were late night discussions about poetry and poets and Abercrombie read him the beginning of a long poem on which he was then working, called 'Zagreus' – of which Marsh says he didn't understand a word – and 'The End of the World' and 'The Staircase', which he described to Brooke as 'magnificent'.

Their distinguished visitor obviously made his opinion of Mrs Abercrombie known to another of his correspondents, D.H. Lawrence. In November 1913, after the Abercrombies, Gibson and Trevelyan had unexpectedly visited him in Italy, Lawrence wrote to Marsh: "We both loved Mrs Abercrombie: she's not a bit like Madonna, neither the Raphael nor Botticelli sort, so you're wrong there, Sir.'[13] Abercrombie returned the visit and stayed with Marsh for five days in London when his host arranged a hectic schedule, which included meeting Lord Dunsany, Diana Manners, Henry James and Mark Gertler. How different Marsh's social scene must have seemed to the simple life of Ryton.

NOTES

1 Quoted in R.P. Beckinsale, *Companion into Gloucestershire*, (Methuen, rev. ed. 1948).
2 Letter, Edward Marsh to Rupert Brooke, quoted in Christopher Hassall's biography, *Edward Marsh: Patron of the Arts*, (Longman, 1959).
3 Catherine Abercrombie, 'Memoirs of a Poet's Wife', *The Listener*, November 15th, 1956.
4 Lascelles Abercrombie's autobiographical essay in John Gawsworth, *Ten Contemporaries; Notes Towards Their Definitive Biography*, (Ernest Benn, 1932).
5 John Gawsworth, ibid.
6 Catherine Abercrombie, ibid.
7 Letter, D.H. Lawrence to Edward Marsh, quoted in G. Zytaruk and J.T. Boulton, *The Letters of D.H. Lawrence, Vol II, June 1913 – October 1916*, (Cambridge University Press, 1981).
8 Catherine Abercrombie, ibid.
9 John Haines, 'Professor Lascelles Abercrombie: A Gloucestershire Poet', *Gloucester Journal*, January 12th, 1935.
10 John Haines, ibid.
11 Catherine Abercrombie, ibid.
12 Letter, Edward Marsh to D.H. Lawrence.
13 Letter, D.H. Lawrence to Edward Marsh, November 1913.

Wilfrid Gibson

Wilfrid Gibson moved to Gloucestershire in 1913 to a part thatched red-brick and timber-built house at the Greenway Cross junction of the Dymock–Tewkesbury road, by the side of the lane to Leddington. Called The Old Nail Shop, it had been the home of the Saddler family, who were actually nail makers.

THE OLD NAIL SHOP

"I dreamt of wings, – and waked to hear
Through the low sloping ceiling clear
The nesting starlings flutter and scratch
Among the rafters of the thatch,
Not twenty inches from my head;
And lay, half dreaming, in my bed,
Watching the far elms, bolt-upright
Black towers of silence in a night
Of stars, square-framed between the sill

Of the casements and the eaves, until
I drowsed, and must have slept a wink . . . .
And wakened to a ceaseless clink
Of hammers ringing on the air . . . .
And, somehow, only half aware,
I'd risen, and crept down the stair,
Bewildered by strange, smoky gloom,
Until I'd reached the living room
That once had been a nail-shed.

And where my hearth had blazed, instead
I saw the nail-forge glowing red;
And, through the strife and smoky glare,
Three dreaming women standing there
With hammers beating red-hot wire
On tinkling anvils, by the fire,
To ten-a-penny nails; and heard –
Though none looked up or breathed a word –
The song each heart sang to the tune
Of hammers, through a Summer's noon,
When they had wrought in that red glow,
Alive, a hundred years ago –
The song of girl and wife and crone,
Sung in the heart of each alone . . . .

The dim-eyed crone with nodding head –
'He's dead; and I'll, too, soon be dead.'

The grave-eyed mother, gaunt with need –
'Another little mouth to feed!'

The black-haired girl, with eyes alight –
'I'll wear the yellow beads tonight'."

The cottage featured again in a small poem, not full of voices as in 'The Golden Room' or the noise of the women in the writer's dream in 'The Old Nail Shop', but lonely and empty:

THE EMPTY COTTAGE

Over the meadows of June
The plovers are crying
All night under the moon
That silvers with ghostly light
The thatch of the little old cottage, so lonely to-night.

Lonely and empty it stands
By the signpost that stretches white hands,
Pointing to far-away lands
Where alone and apart we are lying.

Lonely and empty of all delight
It stands in the blind white night;
And under the thatch there is no one to hark to the crying,
The restless voices of plovers flying and crying
Over the meadows of June,
All night under the moon
Crying . . .

Gibson came to Gloucestershire from London where he had been renting a room above Harold Munro's Poetry Bookshop, and he had married one of Munro's bookshop assistants. He was not a Londoner, but had been born, on October 2nd, 1878, in Hexham, Northumberland, one of the large family of Elizabeth and John Gibson, who was a chemist and an amateur archaeologist and photographer. An early interest in poetry was awakened and encouraged by his half-sister, Elizabeth Cheyne Gibson, who wrote verse.

Wilfrid Gibson

When he came to London in the summer of 1912 to further his career as a poet, John Middleton Murry and Katherine Mansfield, whose magazine *Rhythm* brought together the talents of most of the Georgian poets, found Gibson somewhere to stay and introduced him to the ubiquitous Edward Marsh. Gibson was at this time surviving by reviewing for the *Glasgow Herald*. *Rhythm* nearly closed through mounting debts, until Marsh stepped in to save it. He also found a way to alleviate some of Gibson's problems, by suggesting he be appointed assistant editor and arranged for him to be paid a salary of £1 a week. Marsh paid this out of his own pocket, stipulating that Gibson was not to know he had a benefactor.

By the time the magazine folded in July 1913, Gibson had planned his move to join Abercrombie in Gloucestershire (he originally stayed at The Gallows in the Abercrombies' absence before moving to the Old Nail Shop) and his poetry was becoming quite successful: *Daily Bread* was in its third edition and an American magazine had paid him £10 for his poem 'Flanna Isle'.

Gibson's earliest work was highly romantic, but by 1907 and with the publication of *The Stonefolds* he had begun to find his true style. The urban poor were the subject of his writings; he had been into mines, factories and squalid slums and learned his lessons well, soaking up the way the people spoke and reflecting it in his poetry. After his move to Gloucestershire, the rural poor featured in more of his poetry, especially gypsies and tinkers. He did not portray the travelling people with the usual romanticism of the 'Wraggle-taggle Gipsy' school so prominent at the time, but with a raw reality, as the 'strapping red-haired tinker wench' in the poem 'The Weazel':

THE WEAZEL

A streak of red, the weazel shot
Into the Gallows Wood:
I heard a dying rabbit squeal,
And for a moment stood

Uncertain – then, as by some spell,
Drawn in through briar and thorn,
I followed in the weazel's track,
By clutching brambles torn.

Blindly I followed till I came
To a clearing in the fir;
Then startled suddenly I stopped
As my glance lit on her –

The strapping red-haired tinker wench
Who stood with hands on hips,
And watched me with defiant eyes
And parted panting lips.

At first I only saw her eyes,
Her lips, her hair's fierce red:
And then I saw the huddled man
Who at her feet lay dead.

She saw I saw, yet never blenched,
But still looked straight at me
With parted lips and steady eyes,
And muttered quietly –

I'll go: no need to make a fuss,
Though you've come gey and quick:
You must have smelt the blood – and so
The hangman takes the trick!

But what care I, since I am free
Of him and all his lies,
Since I have stopped his dirty tongue
And shut his sneaky eyes.

What matter though I kick my heels
In air for settling Jim?
The vermin's dead: at least I'll make
A cleaner end than him.

Unlike Abercrombie, who wrote on a grander scale, Gibson was far more a 'poet of the people'. He was recognised as a spokesman for the inarticulate poor, which irked Frost who aspired to be their champion. He was a prolific writer of verse-plays, long and short poems in which he depicted his themes with observation and great imagination, though sometimes showing a certain inconsistency, which more than a few critics have put down to too much writing and too little revising. His later works show a fading of his talents and in some, including the poem about his first meeting with Frost, there is an uncomfortable note-like prose style that Edward Thomas, with his usual perception, had recognised as early as 1912: "At the end of the book [*The Fires, Book I*] we have the feeling that after all, he has been merely embellishing what would have been more effective as pieces of rough prose, extracts from a diary, or even a newspaper."[1]

In 1913, in Dublin, Gibson married Geraldine Audrey Townshend, the daughter of an Irish land agent. The couple had met at Munro's bookshop. They now moved to Gloucestershire and the picturesque thatched Old Nail Shop. Edward Marsh related the news to Rupert Brooke, who was then in the South Seas, on December 13th, 1913:

> Wilfrid is spliced, he writes radiant, he slept here three nights on his way to be married in Dublin – the picture of health and happiness, but completely deserted by the Muse, who seems to have yielded her place to Miss T. with the most deplorable tactfulness.

And there was more news for Brooke the following month:

> Wilfrid writes still in the 7th heaven. I am to go to him for Sunday week in his new cottage near The Gallows.

and after the visit:

> I had a charming Sunday with the Wilfrids who seem flawlessly happy. She is a very nice woman – without physical charm, but very intelligent and as good as gold, evidently a supreme housekeeper. Their cottage is very nice, all with a perfect sense of style – he couldn't have done better for himself.

D.H. Lawrence living in Italy, was also pleased to hear from Marsh of Gibson's impending marriage:

> I must write to Gibson. What an absolutely perfect husband he should make! I think I remember seeing Miss Townsend in the Poetry Bookshop – rather lovable and still, one of those women that make a perfect background. They ought to be happy as birds in a quiet wood . . ."[2]

By July 1914, Brooke had himself been to The Old Nail Shop and, as he related to Russell Loines, he found Gibson still in euphoric mood:

> He is still in a Heaven of delight. I'm going down there again in August. He has been too happy to do *much* work (a state *I* don't quite understand: I can comprehend being too *miserable* to work.)

Fortunately the Muse did return to Gibson and it was to his wife that he wrote, at Dymock, the lovely poem 'For G', the antithesis of 'The Empty Cottage'. The poem was one of a number by Gibson that was set to music by Ivor Gurney.

FOR G

All night under the moon
Plovers are flying

Wilfrid Gibson

Over the dreaming meadows of silvery light,
Over the meadows of June
Flying and crying –
Wandering voices of love in the hush of the night.

All night under the moon
Love, though we're lying
Quietly under the thatch, in the silvery light
Over the meadows of June
Together we're flying –
Rapturous voices of love in the hush of the night.

Of all the Dymock poets, Gibson's poetry showed itself to be the most inspired by the scenes around him: an old cottage, a sunlit beacon, hollyhocks, black elms, the Malvern Hills – and inevitably the wild daffodils:

DAFFODILS

He liked the daffodils; he liked to see
Them nodding in the hedgerows cheerily
Along the dusty lanes as he went by,
Nodding and laughing to a fellow – ay,
Nodding and laughing till you'd almost think
They too enjoyed the jest.
      Without a wink
That solemn butler said it calm and smug,
Deep-voiced as though he talked into a jug –
His lordship says he won't require no more
Crocks riveted or mended till the war
Is over.
    Lord! He'd asked to have a wire
The moment that his lordship should desire
To celebrate the occasion fittingly
By a wild burst of mending crockery,
Like a true Englishman, and hang expense!
He'd had to ask it, though he'd too much sense
To lift a lash or breathe a word before
His lordship's lordship closed the heavy door.
And then he laughed. Lord! but it did him good
That quiet laugh: and somewhere in the wood
Behind the Hall there, a woodpecker laughed
Right out aloud as though he'd gone clean daft –
Right out aloud he laughed, the brazen bird,
As if he didn't care a straw who heard;
But then he'd not his daily bread to earn
By mending crocks.
     And now at every turn

Wilfrid Gibson

The daffodils were laughing quietly,
Nodding and laughing to themselves, as he
Chuckled – *Now there's a patriot, real true-blue!*

It seemed the daffodils enjoyed it too,
The fun of it. He wished that he could see,
Old solemn-mug, them laughing quietly
At him: but then he'd never have a dim
Idea they laughed, and, least of all, at him:
He'd never dream they could be laughing at
A butler.
        'Twould be good to see the fat
Old peach-cheek in his solemn black and starch
Parading in his pompous parlour-march
Across that field of laughing daffodils:
'Twould be a sight to make you skip up hills,
Ay, crutch and all, and never feel your pack,
To see a butler in his starch and black
Among the daffodils ridiculous
As that old bubbly-jock with strut and fuss –
Though that was rather rough upon the bird!
For all his pride, he didn't look absurd
Among the flowers, nor even that black sow
Grunting and grubbing in among them now.
And he was glad he hadn't got a trade
That starched the mother-wit in you and made
A man look silly in a field of flowers.
'Twas better mending crocks, although for hours
You hobbled on – ay, and maybe for days,
Hungry and cold along the muddy ways
Without a job: and even when the sun
Was shining 'twas not altogether fun
To lose the chance of earning a few pence
In these days, though 'twas well he'd got the sense
To see the funny side of things. It cost
You nothing, laughing to yourself: you lost
Far more by going fiddle-faced through life
Looking for trouble.
        He would tell his wife
When he got home; but, lord, she'd never see
What tickled him so mightily, not she!
She'd only look up puzzled-like and say
She didn't wonder at his lordship – nay,
With tripe and trotters at the price they were,
You'd got to count your coppers and take care
Of every farthing.
        Jack would see the fun –

Ay, Jack would see the joke. Jack was his son,
The youngest of the lot: and, man-alive,
'Twas queer that only one of all the five
Had got a twinkle in him – all the rest
Dull as ditchwater to the merriest jest.
Good lads enough they were, their mother's sons,
And they'd all pluck enough to face the guns
Out at the front: they'd got their mother's pluck;
And he was proud of them and wished them luck.
That was no laughing matter – though 'twas well
Maybe if you could crack a joke in hell
And shame the devil. Jack, at least, would fight
As well as any though his heart was light:
Jack was the boy for fighting and for fun;
And he was glad to think he'd got a son
Who, even facing bloody death, would see
That little joke about the crockery,
And chuckle as he charged.
                                    His thoughts dropped back
Through eighteen years, and he again saw Jack
At the old home beneath the Malvern hills,
A little fellow plucking daffodils,
A little fellow who could scarcely walk,
Yet chuckling as he snapped each juicy stalk
And held up every yellow bloom to smell,
Poking his tiny nose into the bell
And sniffing the fresh scent, and chuckling still
As though he'd secrets with each daffodil.
Ay, he could see again the little fellow
In his blue frock among that laughing yellow,
And plovers in their sheeny black and white
Flirting and tumbling in the morning light
About his curly head: he still could see,
Shutting his eyes, as plain as plain could be,
Drift upon drift those long-dead daffodils
Against the far green of the Malvern hills,
Nodding and laughing round his little lad,
As if to see him happy made them glad –
Nodding and laughing . . .
                                    They were nodding now,
The daffodils, and laughing – yet somehow
They didn't seem so merry now . . .
                                    And he
Was fighting in a bloody trench maybe
For very life this minute . . .
                                    They missed Jack,
And he would give them all to have him back.

42

'Daffodils' was published in *Livelihood*, as were 'The Old Nail Shop', and at least five poems obviously composed in Leadon Valley, 'The Plough', 'Strawberries', 'In The Meadow', 'The Elm' and 'The Platelayer'. The next slim volume, *Friends*, was also written during his days in Dymock and poems like 'Tenants', 'Trees', 'Retreat', 'The Orphans', 'The Sweet Tooth', 'The Girl's Song' and 'For G' show the inspiration of his surroundings:

> Suddenly, out of dark and leafy ways,
> We came upon the little house asleep . . .
> (Tenants)

and in 'Retreat':

> . . . He dreamt of flowers in an English lane,
> of hedgerow flowers glistening after rain . . .

The quartet of sonnets, *Home*, is full of love for his wife and their thatched home.

HOME

RETURN

Under the brown bird-haunted eaves of thatch
The hollyhocks in crimson glory burned
Against black timbers and old rosy brick,
And over the green door in clusters thick
Hung tangled passion-flowers when we returned
To our own threshold, and with hand on latch
We stood a moment in the sunset gleam
And looked upon our home as in a dream.

Rapt in a golden glow of still delight,
Together on the threshold in the sun
We stood, rejoicing that we two had won
To this deep golden peace ere day was done,
That over gloomy plain and storm-swept height
We two, O Love, had won to home ere night.

CANDLE-LIGHT

Where through the open window I could see
The supper-table in the golden light
Of tall white candles – brasses glinting bright
On the black gleaming board, and crockery
Coloured like gardens of old Araby –
In your blue gown against the walls of white
You stood adream, and in the starry night
I felt strange loneliness steal over me.

You stood with eyes upon the candle-flame
That kindled your thick hair to burnished gold
As in a golden spell that seemed to hold
My heart's love rapt from me for evermore . . .
And then you stirred, and, opening the door,
Into the starry night you breathed my name.

FIRELIGHT

Against the curtained casement wind and sleet
Rattle and thresh, while snug by our own fire
In dear companionship that naught may tire
We sit – you listening, sewing in your seat,
Half-dreaming in the glow of light and heat,
I reading some old tale of love's desire
That swept on gold wings to disaster dire,
Then sprang re-orient from black defeat.

I close the book, and louder yet the storm
Threshes without. Your busy hands are still,
And on your face and hair the light is warm
As we sit gazing on the coals' red gleam
In a gold glow of happiness, and dream
Diviner dreams the years shall yet fulfil.

MIDNIGHT

Between the midnight pillars of black elms
The old moon hangs, a thin cold amber flame
Over low ghostly mist: a lone snipe wheels
Through shadowy moonshine droning; and there steals
Into my heart a fear without a name
Out of primeval night's resurgent realms,
Unearthly terror chilling me with dread
As I lie waking wide-eyed on the bed.

And then you turn towards me in your sleep,
Murmuring, and with a sigh of deep content
You nestle to my breast, and over me
Steals the warm peace of you; and, all fear spent,
I hold you to me sleeping quietly
Till I too sink in slumber sound and deep.

Like The Gallows, Gibson's home became a centre for British poets. W.H. Davies visited, and stayed too long. He seems to have irritated not just the Gibsons but also the Frosts whom he visited too often, according to the American. "His is the kind of egotism another man's egotism can't put up with" Frost wrote to Sidney Cox. One night the Gibsons seemed to have had enough of their guest and:

". . . limped him over on his wooden leg three miles in the rain from their house to Abercrombies. They hurried poor Davies till the sweat broke out all over him . . . they told him he ought to be proud because he was going to see the greatest poet in England. 'Huh' says Davies, when he arrives in the dooryard dead beat, 'good thing it's the greatest poet in England.' He said it bitterly, but the Gibsons taking him at his word hurried in to tell Abercrombie that by consent of Davies he was the greatest poet in England. But that's what Davies thinks he is himself."[3]

Frost added that Gibson, or his wife at any rate, thought that Gibson himself was the greatest poet.

NOTES

1 Edward Thomas, review in *The Daily Chronicle*, March 9th, 1912.
2 Letter, D.H. Lawrence to Edward Marsh, October 28th, 1913 in G. Zytaruk and J.T. Boulton, *The Letters of D.H. Lawrence, Vol II, June 1913 - October 1916*, (Cambridge University Press, 1981).
3 Letter, Robert Frost to Sidney Cox, September 17th, 1914.

Rupert Brooke, John Drinkwater and New Numbers

Gibson has been staying with Abercrombie, and has got a great idea that he, Abercrombie, Drinkwater and I should combine our publics, and publish from the Abercrombies (Mrs A. does the work) a Volume four times a year.

Rupert Brooke to his mother,
July 11th, 1913

Edward Marsh had brought Gibson and Brooke together in the first place in 1912, though Brooke had such a large and eminent circle of friends that they would undoubtedly have met at some time. Shaw, Barrie, Masefield, de la Mare, Yeats, Hugh Walpole, Ezra Pound, Maynard and Geoffrey Keynes, Chesterton, H.G. Wells, Paul Nash, Sassoon, Henry James and many other leading figures in the arts, letters, theatre and even politics feature in the life of the poet who has been described as 'the handsomest young man in England'.

The first meeting took place in September 1912 on Gibson's first visit to London. Picking up Brooke on the way, Marsh and the Northumberland poet had gone to watch a huge blaze at a London timber yard, which Gibson was later to remember vividly in two poems. It turned out to be an extremely important week, not just because it brought Gibson and Brooke together but it was in this same week that Brooke and Marsh conceived the idea of publishing an anthology of contemporary verse and came up with the name "Georgian Poetry". A lunch was held at short-notice, attended by Gibson, Brooke, Marsh and Harold Munro, editor of *Poetry Review* and about to open his Poetry Bookshop. The anthology, *Georgian Poetry 1911–1912*, was launched and published in November 1912 and brought young poets to a wider public. It included Abercrombie's 'The Sale of Saint Thomas', Brooke's 'The Old Vicarage, Grantchester', 'Dust', 'The Fish', 'Town and Country' and 'Dining-Room Tea', Drinkwater's 'The Fires of God' and three works from Gibson, 'The Hare', 'Geraniums' and 'Devil's Edge'. Other contributors, selected by Marsh, were Gordon Bottomley, G.K. Chesterton, W.H. Davies, de la Mare, James Elroy Flecker, D.H. Lawrence, John Masefield, Harold Munro, T. Sturge Moore, Ronald Ross, Edmund Beale Sargent, James Stephens and R.C. Trevelyan. Marsh prefaced this first anthology of *Georgian Poetry*:

This volume is issued in the belief that English poetry is now once again putting on a new strength and beauty . . . This collection, drawn entirely from the publications of the past two years, may if it is fortunate help the lovers of poetry to realize that we are at the beginning of another "Georgian period" which may take rank in due time with the several great poetic ages of the past.

Rupert Brooke was born in 1887 in Rugby, where his father taught at the famous school. From an early age he was something of a socialite, and seems to have had the ability to attract people who were to become famous: on holiday with his parents at St Ives, for example, he had played on the beach with an equally young Virginia Stephens (Woolf), while at school his closest friends were James Strachey (younger brother of Lytton), Duncan Grant and Geoffrey Keynes. After winning a scholarship to study classics at King's College, Cambridge, he became prominent in the Fabian Society and The Marlowe Dramatic Society, of which he was president. It was here that the legend of Rupert Brooke, that was to grow beyond his poetry with his death in the war, began to take shape. His looks, intellect and considerable youthful charm attracted people, and as a student he had met a staggering list of the great of all generations, ranging from political figures like Ramsay MacDonald to literary celebrities such as Alfred Austin, Thomas Hardy, Hilaire Belloc, H.G. Wells and members of the Bloomsbury Group, through whom he was introduced to Edward Marsh.

Brooke had written poetry at Rugby and at Cambridge he began seeing his work regularly in print, especially in *The Westminster Gazette.* In May 1913 he took a position as touring correspondent for the *Gazette* and set sail for a lengthy tour of North America, the South Seas and Australasia. The night before he sailed a small reception was held for him at a London club, which Gibson attended. Since their first meeting they had become good friends (Brooke affectionately called the Northumberland poet 'Wibson') and had met regularly in London and at Brooke's Grantchester home. It was on this long tour, partly undertaken to get over a love affair, that Brooke received Gibson's letter inviting him to join him, Abercrombie and Drinkwater in the publication of an anthology of their own verse, to be published four times a year. The volume had been through a number of name changes already, including *New Shilling Garland*, after Laurence Binyon's similar *The Shilling Garland* and it was tentatively being called *The Gallows Garland* when Brooke was approached.

The success of Marsh's anthology and of Abercrombie's self-published books of verse, made the new plan very attractive to Brooke, who was then probably the least successful of the quartet and who recognised that the venture could bring him the wider public he wanted.

While in America Brooke discovered the extent of Wilfrid Gibson's public; Abercrombie was already becoming well known in Britain and Drinkwater was forging a name for himself as a poet and in the theatre as a writer, actor and manager. Brooke told his mother in a letter dated July 11th, 1913 that it was a good opportunity for him as his 'public' was smaller than his colleagues'. His reply to Gibson, July 23th, 1913 also showed how conscious he was of this:

> I think the G.G. [*Gallows Garland*] is a great idea. I'm all for amalgamating our four publics, the more that mine is far the smallest! I'm afraid I shall be outwritten by you fluent giants . . .

How ironic that of the four participants in the project, Brooke's contribution was in the long-term to prove the most important.

In the same reply to Gibson of July 23rd, 1913, Brooke wittily illustrated how he saw the contents of the average issue, and his own insignificant contribution to *New Numbers*:

1. Lascelles Abercrombie: Hamam and Mordecai	pp1–78
2. John Drinkwater: The Sonority of God: An Ode	pp79–143
3. W.W. Gibson: Poor Bloody Bill: A Tale	pp144–187
4. Rupert Brooke: Oh Dear! Oh, Dear! A Sonnet	p188
5. Lascelles Abercrombie; Asshur-Bani-Pal and Og King of Bashan	pp189–254
6. John Drinkwater: William Morris: An Appreciation in verse	pp255–377
7. W.W. Gibson: Gas Stoves–No.1 A Brave Poor Thing	pp377–394

Then there would be three hundred pounds profit, divided proportionally to the amount contributed:

W.W.G.	£130. 10.6
L.A.	£94. 7.4
J.D.	£74. 11.11½
R.B.	£0. 10.2½

. . . Anyhow, I'm very pleased and excited about the scheme, and I'll 'come in', right in, without knocking: if ever I write anything again.

Actually it was not Brooke's worth as a contributor that worried many people but Drinkwater's, and for a variety of reasons. There was concern that he was less talented than the other three and more obvious choices were suggested. Edward Marsh thought that James Elroy Flecker, born and living in Cheltenham, or Gordon Bottomley would be preferable. Marsh also noted, in a letter to Brooke in August 1913, that Abercrombie and Gibson were rather uneasy about Drinkwater as a contributor and worried that he might send only poems that he could not sell to other magazines.

John Drinkwater was then making his name in two fields. He was a prolific poet and 'The Fires of God', his contribution to Marsh's anthology, had been well received; Sir Henry Newbolt in a review of *Georgian Poetry* in the magazine *Poetry and Drama*, for March 1913, had called it "one of the most careful and accomplished pieces of writing in the book", though he qualified this by adding "the unfortunate result is that the thought, in so elaborate and finished a form, seems to fail in its due impressiveness."

It was in the theatre, however, that he built his long-lasting reputation. He was born in 1882 at Leytonstone, Essex, and his father, Albert Drinkwater, had turned from teaching to the stage, becoming a professional actor and general manager of the Court, Little and Kingsway theatres in London. Drinkwater followed his father's example, rejecting a safe job (he had joined the Northern Assurance Company as a junior clerk in their Nottingham office on leaving school at 15) to take to the boards.

This was the time of the rise of the provincial repertory movement and Drinkwater joined the Birmingham company, The Pilgrim Players, founded by Barry Jackson and chiefly devoted to English poetic drama. Its first significant production, in 1907, was the 16th century *Interlude of Youth* in which Drinkwater, still then working as an insurance clerk during the day, played a small role as Charity. In October 1912 Jackson began building a theatre on a plot of land behind New Street Station which opened its doors as the Birmingham Repertory Theatre on February 15th, 1913. The first production was *Twelfth Night*, with Felix Aylmer as Orsino and Drinkwater as Malvolio Before the performance Jackson came out in front of the curtain and read an ode, 'Lines For The Opening of The Birmingham Repertory Theatre' composed specially for the occasion by Drinkwater. He had also written a poem, 'The Building' about the construction of the theatre.

Drinkwater not only acted but was appointed the theatre's first manager. Jackson also encouraged him to become a dramatist and he was well rewarded for his faith in the young man, for during his association with Jackson, Drinkwater played some 40 parts and directed around 60 productions. All his earliest successes were at the Birmingham theatre, firstly one act plays like *The Storm* and then in 1918 he scored a considerable success with the full-length play *Abraham Lincoln* which transferred to the Lyric Theatre, Hammersmith, in London where it ran for over a year and did much to establish not only the playwright's reputation but also that of Jackson as an impressario. Drinkwater took the play to America, too, where it played the Cort Theatre in New York with the writer as the Chronicler.

Many of Drinkwater's plays followed the same route from Birmingham to the capital. His *Bird-in-Hand* for instance had been a great success in Birmingham in 1927 — its cast included Peggy Ashcroft and Laurence Olivier who later described his part as "a really moth-eaten juvenile . . . a real wet, we would call him." — before transferring to the Royalty Theatre in Drury Lane and then to New York, starring Jill Esmond. Drinkwater also took productions to Paris where in June 1921 he played Banquo in *Macbeth*, and in 1933 he received the decoration of Knight Commander (Commendatore) of the Order of the Crown of Italy in appreciation of his adaptation of Mussolini's play *Napoleon*.

Abercrombie, Gibson and Marsh made a trip to Birmingham in May 1914 to stay with John Drinkwater and his first wife Kathleen (née Walpole, who acted with the Birmingham company as Cathleen Orford) and to see one of his plays at the Repertory Theatre. Marsh, a regular London theatre-goer, was not overly impressed however, reporting to Brooke, then in the USA, that it "went off quite well – it isn't really good, I'm afraid, and his company is only so-so . . ." This letter of May 10th, 1914 also contained the latest news about his *New Numbers* colleagues and, as ever, showed Marsh's concern about how much work Abercrombie was having to do as a reviewer to earn a living:

> "W. [Gibson] has written a quite excellent poem, 'Hoops', a dialogue between a camel-keeper and a clown at a circus, one of his best . . . Mrs Drinkwater is a cheery hoyden, I rather liked her. Catherine Abercrombie fainted at breakfast on Sunday, and kept her bed, which cast a slight gloom. She is going to have a 3rd child, poor Lascelles will have to review more than ever . . ."

On one occasion, John Drinkwater turned up at The Gallows with a sleeping-bag and announced he wanted to set up camp at the bottom of the garden under the great elms. His 'back to nature' adventure did not last long. On the first night he aroused the family: "something would keep blowing through the hedge at him all the time and scaring him stiff. It was a horse, of course, but as John lived in Birmingham he was not used to night life in the country."[2]

Drinkwater was indeed a 'townie' (as of course were the other members of the Muse Colony) and wrote some extremely effective poems about the urban landscape, such as the Gloucester-inspired 'Lady Street' and 'A Town Window', but he seemed happiest in many respects on country themes, on the villages, hills and people of Gloucestershire, Warwickshire and Oxfordshire. He came to know Gloucestershire and the Cotswolds extremely well.

COTSWOLD LOVE

Blue skies are over Cotswold
And April snows go by,
The lasses turn their ribbons
For April's in the sky,

50

And April is the season
    When Sabbath girls are dressed
From Rodboro' to Camden,
    In all their silken best.

An ankle is a marvel
    When first the buds are brown,
And not a lass but knows it
    From Stow to Gloucester town.
And not a girl goes walking
    Along the Cotswold lanes
But knows men's eyes in April
    Are quicker than their brains.

It's little that it matters,
    So long as you're alive,
If you're eighteen in April,
    Or rising sixty-five,
When April comes to Amberley
    With skies of April blue,
And Cotswold girls are briding
    With slyly tilted shoe.

Eventually he came to live in the county, renting a small cottage in the Cotswold hills, but this was after the war and long after the members of the Muse Colony had gone their separate ways. He also stayed with the Osler family at Upper Farm in Grafton, under the shadow of the Bredon Hills where he collected folk songs in the local public house, The Beckford Inn, and was inspired to write 'At Grafton'.

AT GRAFTON

God laughed when He made Grafton
That's under Bredon Hill,
A jewel in a jewelled Plain.
The seasons work their will
On golden thatch and crumbling stone,
And every soft-lipped breeze
Makes music for the Grafton men
In comfortable trees.

God's beauty over Grafton
Stoke into roof and wall,
And hallowed every paved path
And every lowly stall.
And to a woven wonder
Conspired with one accord
The labour of the servant,
The labour of the Lord.

And momently to Grafton
Comes in from vale and wold
The sound of sheep unshepherded,
The sound of sheep in fold.
And, blown along the bases
Of lands that set their wide
Frank brows to God, comes chanting
The breath of Bristol tide.

Even in some of Drinkwater's urban poems he seemed to be closer to the countryside in spirit and in 'Blackbird' the woods of Dymock were clearly in the poet's mind, as were its orchards in 'Immortality'.

BLACKBIRD

He comes on chosen evenings,
My blackbird bountiful, and sings
Over the gardens of the town
Just at the hour the sun goes down.
His flight across the chimneys thick,
By some divine arithmetic,
Comes to his customary stack,
And couches there his plumage black,
And there he lifts his yellow bill,
Kindled against the sunset, till
These suburbs are like Dymock woods
Where music has her solitudes,
And while he mocks the winter's wrong
Rapt on his pinnacle of song,
Figured above our garden plots
Those are celestial chimney pots.

IMMORTALITY

I

When other beauty governs other lips,
  And snowdrops come to strange and happy springs,
When seas renewed bear yet unbuilded ships,
  And alien hearts know all familiar things,
When frosty nights bring comrades to enjoy
  Sweet hours at hearths where we no longer sit,
When Liverpool is one with dusty Troy,
  And London famed as Attila for wit . . .
How shall it be with you, and you, and you,
  How with us all who have gone greatly here
In friendship, making some delight, some true
  Song in the dark, some story against fear?

Shall song still walk with love, and life be brave,
And we, who were all these, be but the grave?
   II
No; lovers yet shall tell the nightingale
   Sometimes a song that we of old time made,
And gossips gathered at the twilight ale
   Shallsay, "These two were friends", or, "Unafraid
Of bitter thought were those because they loved
   Better than most." And sometimes shall be told
How one, who died in his young beauty, moved,
   And Astrophel, those English hearts of old.
And the new seas shall take the new ships home
   Telling how yet the Dymock orchards stand,
And you shall walk with Julius at Rome,
   And Paul shall be my fellow in the Strand;
There in the midst of all those words shall be
Our names, our ghosts, our immortality.

Despite commanding a larger audience than exists today, publishing poetry was a precarious proposition but Edward Marsh, generous as ever, guaranteed the first two issues of *New Numbers* against loss. The production costs were estimated to be around £15 a volume. Each poet produced a list of possible subscribers, who were then approached and a subscription list drawn up. By December 1913, Marsh was able to tell Brooke that there were already well over 200 subscribers and at the same time give him a gentle nudge to send some verses to Ryton: "England expects from you more than one sonnet" he told him. In the end it was Abercrombie who held things up; he had not finished his poem 'The Olympians' which he wanted to include in the first issue.

A Gloucester printer, The Crypt House Press, printed *New Numbers*, which was bound in grey paper and had a cover price of 2s 6d. Catherine Abercrombie addressed the envelopes to the subscribers and Gibson licked the stamps, making himself ill in the process. The parcels were then carried down to Dymock Post Office where the postmaster, Mr Griffiths, and the Dymock postmen, Charlie Wetson and Jack Brooke, franked the envelopes that were to be sent all over Britain, and some abroad.

The first issue contained 11 poems. Abercrombie had finished 'The Olympians' in time for publication and Gibson contributed a lengthy verse drama, 'Bloodybush Edge' about the meeting of Daft Dick and a tramp at a remote spot on the English-Scottish border. Brooke contributed four poems: 'Sonnet', 'A Memory', 'One Day' and 'Mutability', all penned in the South Seas the previous year. Drinkwater was represented by five poems: 'The Poet to his Mistress', 'The New Miracle', 'The Boundaries', 'Memory' and 'A Town Window'.

A TOWN WINDOW

Beyond my window in the night
    Is but a drab inglorious street,
Yet there the frost and clear starlight
    As over Warwick woods are sweet.

Under the grey drift of the town
    The crocus works among the mould
As eagerly as those that crown
    The Warwick spring in flame and gold.

And when the tramway down the hill
    Across the cobbles moans and rings,
There is about my window-sill
    The tumult of a thousand wings.

Rupert Brooke received the news of the first issue from an excited Edward Marsh in a letter dated March 9th, 1914: "*N.N.* is out! It's very good, the shape, print and appearance quite excellent." The press received it well and *The Times* published a very favourable review, singling out Abercrombie's verse drama for particular praise and quoting in full Brooke's 'Sonnet'.[3]

SONNET

(Suggested by some of the Proceedings of the
Society for Psychical Research)

Not with vain tears, when we're beyond the sun,
    We'll beat on the substantial doors, nor tread
    Those dusty high-roads of the aimless dead
Plaintive for Earth; but rather turn and run
Down some close-covered by-way of the air;
    Some low sweet alley between wind and wind,
    Stoop under faint gleams, thread the shadows, find
Some whispering ghost-forgotten nook, and there
Spend in pure converse our eternal day;
    Think each in each, immediately wise;
Learn all we lacked before; hear, know, and say
    What this tumultuous body now denies;
And feel, who have laid our groping hands away;
    And see, no longer blinded by our eyes.

One unexpected piece of publicity occurred at the first night of a play, *Outcasts*, at Wyndham's Theatre in London, which Brooke attended. Gerald du Maurier was supposed to be seen reading a 'French obscene journal', but to

Brooke's amusement he actually held a copy of *New Numbers*.

Brooke was still abroad when the first issue of *New Numbers* was published but he returned to Britain in June, 1914 and in July stayed at The Old Nail Shop with the Gibsons where he joined in the planning of subsequent issues. During his trip overseas he had not spent his time idly but had written a number of new works, mostly sonnets written in the South Seas islands where he had fallen in love with a Tahitian called Toatamata. The sonnet known as 'Psychical Research' was one of the South Seas compositions, as was the unusual 'Heaven'. The latter he had originally sent to Marsh who was staying with the Gibsons and he thought it was 'brilliantly amusing' and 'beautiful'. Marsh was sure that if included in *New Numbers* it would lead to cancelled subscriptions. Presumably it was decided to risk the wrath of *New Numbers'* clerical subscribers, for 'Heaven' appeared in the second issue, Brooke's only contribution to that volume.

HEAVEN

Fish (fly-replete, in depth of June,
Dawdling away their wat'ry noon)
Ponder deep wisdom, dark or clear,
Each secret fishy hope or fear.
Fish say, they have their Stream and Pond;
But is there anything Beyond?
This life cannot be All, they swear,
For how unpleasant, if it were!
One may not doubt that, somehow, Good
Shall come of Water and of Mud;
And, sure, the reverent eye must see
A Purpose in Liquidity.
We darkly know, by Faith we cry,
The future is not Wholly Dry.
Mud unto mud! – Death eddies near –
Not here the appointed End, not here!
But somewhere, beyond Space and Time,
Is wetter water, slimier slime!
And there (they trust) there swimmeth One
Who swam ere rivers were begun,
Immense, of fishy form and mind,
Squamous, omnipotent, and kind;
And under that Almighty Fin,
The littlest fish may enter in.
Oh! never fly conceals a hook,
Fish say, in the Eternal Brook,
But more than mundane weeds are there,

> And mud, celestially fair;
> Fat caterpillars drift around
> And Paradisal grubs are found;
> Unfading moths, immortal flies,
> And the worm that never dies.
> And in that Heaven of all their wish,
> There shall be no more land, say fish.

Despite Brooke's small contribution to the second issue, the quartet seemed to have divided the first four issues to ensure that they were given equal prominence. In turn they were, for example, given prime position in the contents list of each issue: in number one Gibson led the contents, in number two it was Abercrombie, Brooke in the third and Drinkwater the fourth. Their individual contributions were varied, though Abercrombie restricted himself to one lengthy verse drama for each issue – 'The Olympians' (1), 'The End of the World' (2), 'The Innocent' (3) and 'The Staircase' (4) – and included none of his shorter poems. Brooke's single poem in number two was compensated by the inclusion of five works in number three including 'The Great Lover':

THE GREAT LOVER

> I have been so great a lover: filled my days
> So proudly with the splendour of Love's praise,
> The pain, the calm, and the astonishment,
> Desire illimitable, and still content,
> And all dear names men use, to cheat despair,
> For the perplexed and viewless streams that bear
> Our hearts at random down the dark of life.
> Now, ere the unthinking silence on that strife
> Steals down, I would cheat drowsy Death so far,
> My night shall be remembered for a star
> That outshone all the suns of all men's days.
> Shall I not crown them with immortal praise
> Whom I have loved, who have given me, dared with
>   me
> High secrets, and in darkness knelt to see
> The inenarrable godhead of delight?
> Love is a flame:—we have beaconed the world's
>   night.
> A city:—and we have built it, these and I.
> An emperor:—we have taught the world to die.
> So, for their sakes I loved, ere I go hence,
> And the high cause of Love's magnificence,
> And to keep loyalties young, I'll write those names

Golden for ever, eagles, crying flames,
And set them as a banner, that men may know,
To dare the generations, burn, and blow
Out on the wind of Time, shining and streaming. . . .
These I have loved:
    White plates and cups, clean-gleaming,
Ringed with blue lines; and feathery, faery dust;
Wet roofs, beneath the lamp-light; the strong crust
Of friendly bread; and many-tasting food;
Rainbows; and the blue bitter smoke of wood;
And radiant raindrops couching in cool flowers;
And flowers themselves, that sway through sunny
 hours,
Dreaming of moths that drink them under the moon;
Then, the cool kindliness of sheets, that soon
Smooth away trouble; and the rough male kiss
Of blankets; grainy wood; live hair that is
Shining and free; blue-massing clouds; the keen
Unpassioned beauty of a great machine;
The benison of hot water; furs to touch;
The good smell of old clothes; and others such—
The comfortable smell of friendly fingers,
Hair's fragrance, and the musty reek that lingers
About dead leaves and last year's ferns. . . .
      Dear names,
And thousand other throng to me! Royal flames;
Sweet water's dimpling laugh from tap or spring;
Holes in the ground; and voices that do sing;
Voices in laughter, too; and body's pain,
Soon turned to peace; and the deep-panting train;
Firm sands; the little dulling edge of foam
That browns and dwindles as the wave goes home;
And washen stones, gay for an hour; the cold
Graveness of iron; moist black earthen mould;
Sleep; and high places; footprints in the dew;
And oaks; and brown horse-chestnuts, glossy-new;
And new-peeled sticks; and shining pools on grass;—
All these have been my loves. And these shall pass,
Whatever passes not, in the great hour,
Nor all my passion, all my prayers, have power
To hold them with me through the gate of Death.
They'll play deserter, turn with the traitor breath,
Break the high bond we made, and sell Love's trust
And sacramented covenant to the dust.
——Oh, never a doubt but, somewhere, I shall wake,
And give what's left of love again, and make
New friends, now strangers. . . .

> But the best I've known
> Stays here, and changes, breaks, grows old, is blown
> About the winds of the world, and fades from brains
> Of living men, and dies.
> Nothing remains.
>
> O dear my loves, O faithless, once again
> This one last gift I give: that after men
> Shall know, and later lovers, far-removed,
> Praise you, 'All these were lovely'; say, 'He loved.'

Mataiea, 1914

For the fourth issue of *New Numbers* Brooke contributed 'The Treasure' and the five-part '1914'. If for nothing else, it was for this first publication of '1914' that *New Numbers* has such an important place in the history of English poetry, for it was as much on these sonnets, in particular the fifth, 'The Soldier', as well as the oft-quoted 'Old Vicarage, Grantchester' that Brooke's popular reputation rests.

THE SOLDIER

> If I should die, think only this of me:
>   That there's some corner of a foreign field
> That is forever England. There shall be
>   In that rich earth a richer dust concealed
> A dust whom England bore, shaped, made aware,
>   Gave, once, her flowers to love, her ways to roam,
> A body of England's, breathing English air,
>   Washed by the rivers, blast by suns of home.
>
> And think, this heart, all evil shed away,
>   A pulse in the eternal mind, no less
> Gives somewhere back the thoughts by England given;
> Her sights and sounds; dreams happy as her day;
>   And laughter, learnt of friends; and gentleness,
>   In hearts of peace, under an English heaven.

Brooke sent Russell Loines some copies of the magazine on July 6th, 1914, enclosing a letter in which he wrote: "The thing is going well; about seven or eight hundred of each number which pays expenses very easily, and leaves a good bit for division. It goes on selling steadily, & I suppose it always will – I mean the back numbers will continue to go off. I hope so, for the more it's sold, the more poetry, & less reviews, Abercrombie & Gibson can write & the better for the world . . ." Twelve days later, he sent out more copies, this time to Mrs Chauncey Wells:

There's some awfully good Abercrombie in it: and we're rather proud of the whole thing. Some of the things I read you in April just missed this number and will appear in the next: and I should have twenty or thirty pages in the fourth number. We have already more than enough subscriptions to cover expenses, and there's also the sale of odd copies – so all seems flourishing . . .

Number four was the final issue. The restrictions caused by the war, not least the lack of paper and the growing cost of printing, were contributory factors behind its demise, but it was the death of Brooke that signalled the end.

NEW NUMBERS

Number One

GIBSON: Bloodybush Edge
BROOKE: Sonnet (Psychical Research)
      A Memory
      One Day
      Mutability
ABERCROMBIE: The Olympians
DRINKWATER: The Poet to his Mistress
      The New Miracle
      The Boundaries
      A Town Window
      Memory

Number Two

ABERCROMBIE: The End of the World
DRINKWATER: Love's House
BROOKE: Heaven
GIBSON: A Catch for Singing
      The Tram
      The Greeting
      On Hampstead Heath
      The Ice
      The Goose

Number Three

BROOKE: Tiara Tahiti
      Retrospect
      The Great Lover
      Waikiki
      Hauntings

DRINKWATER: The Storm
GIBSON: Wheels
      Hoops
ABERCROMBIE: The Innocents

Number Four

DRINKWATER: The Carver in Stone
BROOKE: The Treasure
      1914 I Peace
      II Safety
      III The Dead
      IV The Dead
      V The Soldier
ABERCROMBIE: The Staircase
GIBSON: The Orphans
      The Pessimist
      Girl's Song
      The Old Nail Shop
      The Shaft

NOTES

1   Sir Laurence Olivier, *Confessions of an Actor*, (Weidenfeld & Nicolson, 1982).
2   Catherine Abercrombie, 'Memoirs of a Poet's Wife', *The Listener*, November 15th, 1956.
3   The sonnet was inspired by a paper on 'Recent Results in Psychical Research' that Brooke had heard read by its author, A.C. Pigon, King's Don in Political Economy, many years earlier at The Dickinson Society, King's College, Cambridge.

Robert Frost

In 1913 Robert Frost called on Wilfrid Gibson in his 'London garret' as part of his campaign to solicit support for his *North of Boston*, which was yet to be published, a tactic he had successfully used before the publication of *A Boy's Will*. Gibson recalled the occasion many years later, in 1947.

THE FIRST MEETING

One evening, while in my London garret,
I worked upon a piece of Northern verse
About the Border-raiders, and was rapt
In my visions of my native countryside,
As my mind rambled over starlet fells –
Catching the thud of hoofs across the heath
And watching flaring flames of burning byres –
A sudden sharp tap-tapping at the door
Startled me; and, somewhat reluctantly,
I rose and opened it: and then was told
A stranger, an American, called Frost,
Had turned up, and would like to have a word
With me. I put my manuscript aside;
And, when he was shewn in, though still my thoughts
Hung around 'Bloody Bush Edge' for a brief while,
It wasn't long before the two of us
Were chatting in a close companionship;
And I had lost the last shred of regret
That I'd been interrupted in the business
Of my comparatively inconsequential work;
As I sat listening to Frost's racy speech
And relishing his pithy commentaries
On this and that. And when, too soon he rose
To leave, I gladly took from him a sheaf
Of verse he, diffidently, handed me;
Saying he'd be obliged if I would bother
To look it through, and let him have a word
Of what I thought of it . . .
. . . Thirty-five years –
Years of disastrous and dismayed distraction –
Have passed since then; and even the old house
Within whose garret we first met, was bombed
Into oblivion in the days of war:
Yet, though the wide waste of the Atlantic severs

61

Two old friends, who will hardly chance to meet
Again in this world, it appears to me
Incredible to think that "North of Boston" –
A work that, with direct colloquial vigour,
Expressed the essential facts of like,
While, with perceptive sensibility
Infusing them with subtle implications
Of all our human hopes and fears, that give
To its New Englanders a universal
Significance – should ever have been for me
A sheaf of unfamiliar verse; and still
Stranger that Frost, my vitalising friend,
Was ever someone I had never met –
Poems and a poet, that would seem to have been
The very inspiration of my life!

Through Gibson, Frost was introduced to Abercrombie who had already been living in Ryton for a couple of years. Abercrombie and Gibson, who was planning to join him in Gloucestershire, both insisted that the American should move his family from their present bungalow in Beaconsfield and come to the Leadon Valley to see some real English countryside. On March 26th, 1914, Frost wrote to Sidney Cox:

> I have no friend here like Wilfrid Gibson whom I am going to join in Gloucestershire next week. We bid a long farewell to London to be near him and Lascelles Abercrombie. The cottage is already found for us. Iddens it is called – in Ledington Ledbury. You must address us there from now on. I don't know but I suppose we shall sleep under thatch. Those other poets do.

And years later, back in America, he told Louis Mertins:

> These were the friends we had made: there was the urge to be with those who spoke our language and understood our thoughts . . . We had never lived among poets before, working poets.[1]

The six Frosts – Robert and his wife Elinor and their four children, Lesley, Carol, Irma and Marjorie – travelled by train to Dymock where they were met by the Abercrombies and Gibsons. They had rented two large carriages and the three families set out to tour the area like visiting royalty. Their journey included a brief stop at Gibson's cottage and Leddington before returning to Dymock village and on to Ryton where the Americans were to stay temporarily with the Abercrombies at The Gallows.

The cottage that had been found for the Frosts at Leddington was not, as he had surmised, thatched but it was picturesque and old and the Americans rented it for a year, paying the whole year's rent of $50 in advance. Little Iddens, with its brick floor, open beams, old-fashioned stove, black and white timber frame infilled with painted brick and an old iron pump for water was idyllic, situated along a very narrow lane amid the fields and orchards with fine views of May Hill in the distance. It had a vegetable garden at the front with a weeping ash and a bay tree, a walnut in a yard of cobbles and grass behind, a yew on the roadside and an orchard on the other.

It was small, with five rooms and only basic amenities, but greatly preferred by the poet to the Beaconsfield house, which he nicknamed "The Bunghole".

> . . . let me try what I can say in a few words about where we are. The important thing to us is that we are near Gibson; we are far from any town. We are on a lane where no automobiles come. We can go almost anywhere we wish on wavering footpaths through the fields. The fields are so small and the trees so numerous along the hedges that, as my friend Thomas says in the loveliest book on spring in England,[2] you may think from a little distance that the country was solid wood.

The letter, to Sidney Cox and dated May 18th, 1914, continues:

> This is a great change from Beaconsfield which was merely suburban. We are now in the country, the cider country, where we have to keep a barrel of cider for our visitors and our hired help or we will have no visitors nor hired help. So we are in the way of adding drink to cigarette smoking in the record of our sins.

Frost's children seem to have settled quickly into life in rural Gloucestershire, though they all suffered from homesickness and hated the English education system so much that Elinor Frost took over teaching them. Their friend, the Gloucester solicitor John Haines, remembered Elinor and the children as charming and very easy to get on with, interested in everything they saw and were told:

> Lesley at 15 was very nearly grown up and well educated and very handsome. I fancy she read a great deal. The youngest girl (Marjorie) was very quiet and shy. Irma and Carol were most delightful children, very talkative and lively. Irma looked fragile but was lively enough and was the one who asked the most questions about everything. She was the most American of the four, I thought, but Carol might have been an English boy except for his ability to 'jerk' stones across the little River Leadon, at which he licked me hollow, as at least one of the girls; and RF himself was prodigious at it.[3]

The Frosts' rural upbringing in the States stood them good stead in Gloucestershire, and the children became keen gardeners; according to local people they produced exceptional vegetables at Little Iddens. Carol Frost became a favourite with the aptly named Mrs Farmer, who lived at the neighbouring Glyn Iddens, and he was allowed to join her fruit pickers. His father, too, knew the joy and the sheer exhaustion of the fruit harvest; the ache of the instep arch from too long on the picker's ladder in 'After Apple-Picking' is something he must have known through personal experience:

AFTER APPLE-PICKING

My long two-pointed ladder's sticking through a tree
Toward heaven still,
And there's a barrel that I didn't fill
Beside it, and there may be two or three
Apples I didn't pick upon some bough.
But I am done with apple-picking now.
Essence of winter sleep is on the night,
The scent of apples: I am drowsing off.
I cannot rub the strangeness from my sight
I got from looking through a pane of glass
I skimmed this morning from the drinking trough
And held against the world of hoary grass.
It melted, and I let it fall and break.
But I was well
Upon my way to sleep before it fell,
And I could tell
What form my dreaming was about to take.
Magnified apples appear and disappear,
Stem end and blossom end,
And every fleck of russet showing clear.
My instep arch not only keeps the ache,
It keeps the pressure of a ladder-round.
I feel the ladder sway as the boughs bend.
And I keep hearing from the cellar bin
The rumbling sound
Of load on load of apples coming in.
For I have had too much
Of apple-picking: I am overtired
Of the great harvest I myself desired.
There were ten thousand thousand fruit to touch,
Cherish in hand, lift down, and not let fall.
For all
That struck the earth,
No matter if not bruised or spiked with stubble,
Went sure to the cider-apple heap
As of no worth.
One can see what will trouble
This sleep of mine, whatever sleep it is.
Were he not gone,
The woodchuck could say whether it's like his
Long sleep, as I describe its coming on,
Or just some human sleep.

1. *Above: Lascelles and Catherine Abercrombie with their sons David and Michael at Ryton. Reproduced by permission of Jeff Cooper.*

2. *Right: Lascelles Abercrombie and his sons David and Michael, outside The Gallows, Ryton. Reproduced by permission of Jeff Cooper.*

3. Top: Robert Frost, circa 1915. Copyright Hulton-Deutsch.

4. Left: Robert Frost on his arrival in England in 1957, when he revisited Dymock. Copyright Hulton-Deutsch.

5. Above: Wilfrid Gibson and his wife Geraldine at the doorway of The Old Nail Shop.

6. Right: Wilfrid Gibson.

7. Below: Wilfrid Gibson at the gate to The Old Nail Shop.

8. Rupert Brooke, 1913. Copyright Hulton-Deutsch.

9. John Drinkwater.

10. Edward Thomas.
Copyright Hulton-Deutsch.

11. *Above: Sir
Edward Marsh
KCVO, on receiving
his knighthood in 1937.
Copyright Hulton-
Deutsch.*

12. *Left: W.H. Davies
by E.O. Hoppé.
Copyright Hulton-
Deutsch.*

*13. The Old Nail Shop,
home of Wilfrid Gibson.*

*14. The road from the
home of Wilfrid Gibson
to that of Robert Frost.*

*15. Little Iddens, home
of Robert Frost 1914.*

16. Top: Glyn Iddens,
where Eleanor Farjeon
had rooms.

17. Right: Ryton Firs.
The subject of one of
Lascelles Abercrombie's
best known poems.

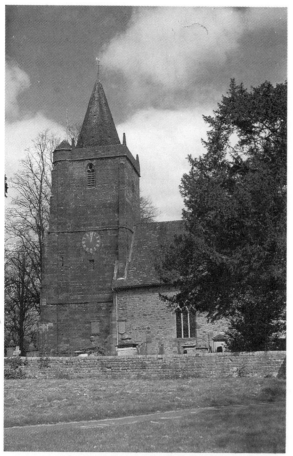

18. Top: Dymock Church.

19. Bottom: May Hill.

Frost later recalled in a letter to John Haines in 1925 that he had heard Mrs Farmer had poisoned the whole apple orchard her husband had planted at Glyn Iddens so as to keep it from coming into the possession of her brother, from whom they rented the farm and who was trying to evict her.

For Carol Frost, there was an additional benefit to be gained from toiling in the orchard and picking the precious fruit – hearty meals in the farmhouse kitchen. Elinor Frost was not a natural housekeeper and meal times were haphazard affairs; when the children grew hungry they helped themselves to bread, fruit or cold rice from bowls in the small kitchen. Often as midday approached she would take a bucket of potatoes into the field beside the house and sit on the grass and peel them (without water, as Helen Thomas, her opposite when it came to housekeeping, was 'astonished' to see) – her only concession to a hot meal. However, she kept her metal coffee pot on the stove all day long, a practice she continued when the Frosts moved later in the year to The Gallows. Catherine Abercrombie remarked that "she 'imbibed' more coffee in the day than I did in a month".

Robert Frost seems to have been no better at providing meals for his family. Fearful lest the war should cause a food shortage, he went into Ledbury one day to stock up and filled part of the small living room with his purchases: packets of Shredded Wheat, tins of rather cheap sugary biscuits and boxes of highly-scented soap.

Bedtimes at Little Iddens were equally haphazard. The Frosts were not ruled by the clock and seem to have had no set times for meals or bed. The children went to bed when they felt like it; it was more important for a child to go for a walk in the dark than to have an unbroken night's rest.

Frost knew more of country life than any of his literary colleagues. Born in San Francisco in 1874, he had, after two years at Harvard University, turned to farming in New Hampshire, though by 1906 he had almost forsaken the farm for a teaching job at a local school. At the same time he was writing, but having little success in getting his work into print. In 1912 he sold the farm and the Frosts came to England. It was a wise move for both *A Boy's Will* and, more important, *North of Boston* were first published in Britain.

In appearance and speech he was far from the archetypal aesthete, as Eleanor Farjeon, who came to stay at Glyn Iddens in the summer of 1914, discovered:

> I remember his figure as middle-sized and compact, his manner friendly and undemonstrative; he looked at you directly, his talk was shrewd and speculative, withholding nothing and derived from nobody but himself. His New England speech came readily and leisurely, and of all the writers of worth whom I had met he spoke with the least sophistication.[4]

Helen Thomas also met Robert Frost for the first time at Leddington, when the Thomases came to stay in 1914, though her husband had become a close friend of the American poet in London the previous winter.

> Robert was a thickset man, not as tall as Edward, with a shock of grey hair. His face was tanned and weatherbeaten and his features powerful. His eyes, shaded by bushy, grey eyebrows, were blue and clear. It was a striking and pleasing face.[5]

Frost's poetry was from the outset far more derivative from the country than that of most of his colleagues, expressed in simple language and, as he later explained to Edward Thomas, the 'cadence' of speech of the common man. In *Mountain Interval*, published after his return to the States, we find poems like 'Putting in the Seed' and 'The Cow at Apple Time' that could have been inspired as much by the fields and orchards of Leddington as of New Hampshire.

THE COW AT APPLE TIME

Something inspires the only cow of late
To make no more of a wall than an open gate,
And think no more of wall-builders than fools.
Her face is flecked with pomace and she drools
A cider syrup. Having tasted fruit,
She scorns a pasture withering to the root.
She runs from tree to tree where lie and sweeten
The windfalls spiked with stubble and worm-eaten.
She leaves them bitten when she has to fly.
She bellows on a knoll against the sky.
Her udder shrivels and the milk goes dry.

PUTTING IN THE SEED

You come to fetch me from my work tonight
When supper's on the table, and we'll see
If I can leave off burying the white
Soft petals fallen from the apple tree
(Soft petals, yes, but not so barren quite,
Mingled with these, smooth bean and wrinkled pea;)
And go along with you ere you lose sight
Of what you came for and become like me,
Slave to a springtime passion for the earth.
How Love burns through the Putting in the Seed
On through the watching for that early birth
When, just as the soil tarnishes with weed,
The sturdy seedling with arched body comes
Shouldering its way and shedding the earth crumbs.

In Beaconsfield, Elinor Frost had come to resent the frequent visits of poets and writers, so there was a certain respite to be enjoyed at remote Leddington. She was not robust and tired quickly, so guests were an extra burden. Visitors did find their way to the remote cottage, but in most cases they were invited guests like John Haines, with whom Frost struck up what was to become a life-long friendship.

> I don't believe I had one uneasy moment with you the other day from the moment I saw you throw the train car door open. I should think you were the kind of person I could ask over here to sprawl – not call. I object to callers more and more in my old age. In my wife's present state of health I have to do some of the meals (so to call them), but you won't mind that will you? And you will overlook some other things if we can laze and talk for a day. You must come out on the early train and go on the late.[6]

Abercrombie had suggested to Haines that he meet Frost on one of his 'botanising' expeditions.

> It was in one of the flowery country lanes north of Dymock that I met a thick-set man of my own age, and medium height, with blue eyes and a beautiful sensitive mouth, and asked him if he knew where a Mr Robert Frost lived. He replied, with a smile, as I half suspected, that he himself was Robert Frost, and that his cottage was only a few yards away. I had been botanising, and was carrying my vasculum, or collecting tin, and Robert Frost's eyes froze on to that tin, whilst he explained that he also was a botanist, as indeed I had known from his poetry. With this link between us, for something like a year we met and wandered over May Hill, the Leadon Valley, and the ridges of the Cotswolds, hunting flowers together, and talking ceaselessly of poets and poetry . . .

> . . . To listen to Robert Frost on poetry, his own and that of others, was a perpetual joy to me, especially when, seated after a long walk, in the quiet of the cottage, he would sit up to the small hours of the morning pouring forth his views in a steady stream of unforgettable eloquence; for, just as his verse, as was his boast, had in it all the conversational tones of natural speech, so had his actual speech the unmistakeable ring of poetry and the knowledge of, and the power to create the beauty that can be wrought from words was at the core of his spiritual being, so that he could never write or talk seriously save in the tones and cadences of a poet.[7]

Together, and later with Edward Thomas when he came to stay nearby, they walked the fields and lanes, the two Englishmen educating the American in the names of the flowers and birds they discovered on their way. On one such walk, Edward Thomas and Robert Frost had a 'mystical' experience that prompted Frost to write later:

Robert Frost

IRIS BY NIGHT

One misty evening, one another's guide,
We two were groping down a Malvern side
The last wet fields and dripping hedges home.
There came a moment of confusing lights,
Such as according to belief in Rome
Were seen of old at Memphis on the heights
Before the fragments of a former sun
Could concentrate anew and rise as one.
Light was a paste of pigment in our eyes.
And there was a moon and then a scene
So watery as to seem submarine;
In which we two stood saturated, drowned.
The clover-mingled rowan on the ground
Had taken all the water it could as dew,
And still the air was saturated too,
Its airy pressure turned to water weight.
Then a small rainbow like a trellis gate,
A very small moon-made prismatic bow,
Stood closely over us through which to go.
And then we were vouchsafed the miracle
That never yet to other two befell
And I alone of us have lived to tell.
A wonder! Bow and rainbow as it bent,
Instead of moving with us as we went
(To keep the pots of gold from being found),
It lifted from its dewy pediment
Its two mote-swimming many coloured ends
And gathered them together in a ring.
And we stood in it softly circled round
From all division time or foe can bring
In a relation of elected friends.

Elinor Frost's decision to teach her children herself led to an interesting project, the production of their own magazine. This was begun in Beaconsfield, continued at Little Iddens and the last 'issue' produced in America after their return. The magazine was called *The Bouquet* and comprised poems, stories, riddles and illustrations. Editor-in-chief was Lesley Frost, who typed the text on a small typewriter her father had brought with him from New Hampshire, using carbon paper to produce additional copies. Six issues were produced: number one came out in April 1914 and was begun during a visit by Edward Thomas and his son Merfyn, who joined Lesley, Carol and Irma Frost as a contributor.

By June 1914, the Frosts were ensconced at Little Iddens and, during another visit by Thomas and his son, a second issue was produced, followed by two others that year, in June and September. The fifth issue, dated June 1915, was begun in Gloucestershire and finished in America and there is a sixth issue of June 1916 that was purely American. Surviving copies of all six issues of *The Bouquet* are in the Bartlett Collection, Virginia and a copy of one issue is on display in Dymock Church.

Frost made an interesting contribution to the children's project, a short four stanza poem called 'Pea-sticks', an earlier form of his poem 'Pea Brush'.

PEA BRUSH

I walked down alone Sunday after church
   To the place where John has been cutting trees,
To see for myself about the birch
   He said I could have to bush my peas.

The sun in the new-cut narrow gap
   Was hot enough for the first of May,
And stifling hot with the odor of sap
   From stumps still bleeding their life away.

The frogs that were peeping a thousand shrill
   Wherever the ground was low and wet,
The minute they heard my step went still
   To watch me and see what I came to get.

Birch boughs enough piled everywhere! –
   All fresh and sound from the recent axe
Time someone came with cart and pair
   And got them off the wild flowers' backs.

They might be good for garden things
   To curl a little finger round,
The same as you seize cat's-cradle strings.
   And lift themselves up off the ground.

Small good to anything growing wild,
   They were crooking many a trillium
That had budded before the boughs were piled
   And since it was coming up had to come.

Thomas too contributed poems to the children's magazine, including 'The Combe':

Robert Frost

THE COMBE

The Combe was ever dark, ancient and dark.
Its mouth is stopped with bramble, thorn, and briar;
And no one scrambles over the sliding chalk
By beech and yew and perishing juniper
Down the half precipices of its sides, with roots
And rabbit holes for steps. The sun of Winter,
The moon of Summer, and all the singing birds
Except the missel-thrush that loves juniper,
And quite shut out. But far more ancient and dark
The Combe looks since they killed the badger there,
Dug him out and gave him to the hounds,
That most ancient Briton of English beasts.

In mid-September the Frosts left Little Iddens and moved to The Gallows, where they occupied the three bedrooms over the kitchen and pantry in the large annexe to the rear of the house. It was these rooms they had occupied when they first came to Dymock earlier the same year. Quite why they moved from Little Iddens has never been fully explained; it certainly wasn't because of the rent, for they paid this in advance for a whole year and while at The Gallows they used the old cottage at Leddington as a store for their belongings. The thought of spending the winter in the poorly heated Little Iddens was most likely a major factor, as was the problem of squeezing a family of four children and two adults into the small cottage – not a problem in the hot summer when they spent most of the days outside but a real problem in the winter months. No doubt the Frosts and the Abercrombies also enjoyed sharing expenses at a time when the war was making the future of poetry publishing very uncertain.

The two families mixed well, though Catherine Abercrombie found the lively Frost children, increasingly homesick for America, a little difficult to handle. Their inability to mix with local children was affecting the relationship with neighbours. Rumours that Frost, with his strange New England accent and unusual ways, was of all things a spy for the Kaiser did not help. Frost's reputation was not helped by some confusion over a Dutchman called Van Doorn, who had visited Ryton and, with his German-sounding accent and long black beard, must have appeared the archetypal spy.

As writers we are a little mysterious to the peasant kind. They have had the police busy about us . . .

Frost wrote to Sidney Cox from Ryton on September 17th, 1914, and many years later he told Louis Mertins:

. . . in the early days of the war they got to spreading stories about me, saying I was a German spy, at least sympathizer. This was as it happened. They told that I would go down to the cellar, and shut myself up to sing German songs. They had no knowledge that 'God Save The King' had for tune an old German drinking song. The provincials would talk around me. They watched every move I made, day and night. They even got the constabulary down to investigate me.[8]

It wasn't only the American who was suspected of being an enemy agent. Thomas, too, was regarded with some suspicion, and even Abercrombie, with his good connections with the local gentry, did not escape the over fertile imaginations of the locals:

They suspected Abercrombie because a year ago he entertained a strange artist lady who goes about the country on her hands and knees because she's paralyzed or thinks she is. Sometimes she rides in a pony cart. She has to be lifted in and out of that. She gets anybody to pick her up off the ground. She is all wasted to nothing. But as country folk remember she might well have been a German officer in disguise.[9]

Poets being taken for spies was nothing new. When Coleridge and Wordsworth were living in Nether Stowey in Somerset in 1796, the suspicions that they were French spies were so strong that a Home Office investigator was sent from London. He thought them harmless cranks. In 1916, D.H. Lawrence and his German wife were also investigated when they lived at Zennor in Cornwall, and the following year, their cottage was searched by the police.

Generally however the occupants of The Gallows felt a million miles away from the war, though Frost did once write that they experienced a certain fear, but of what they were not sure. There was also the night when a neighbour, Mrs Badney, knocked on the door of The Gallows to tell them that the Germans had landed in Portsmouth and that Ledbury 'was upside-down' – she had in fact confused the story of an American ship coming to Britain to bring Christmas gifts (and with remarkable fairness going on to do the same in Belgium, France and Germany.)

While Frost loved Little Iddens, The Gallows seemed to hold a special place in his heart, perhaps because it was thatched. His feelings many years later on hearing that the cottage at Ryton had fallen into ruin are clear from the poem 'The Thatch', first published in *West-running Brook* in 1928. The poem also shows another side to Frost's character; he was subject to deep depressions and suicidal tendencies – on one occasion drawing a revolver to show his seriousness – but also suffered from guilt for the grief he caused his wife during these bad spells.

71

Robert Frost

THE THATCH

Out alone in the winter rain,
Intent on giving and taking pain.
But never was I far out of sight
Of a certain upper-window light.
The light was what it was all about:
I would not go in till the light went out;
It would not go out till I came in.
Well, we should see which one would win,
We should see which one would be first to yield.
The world was a black invisible field.
The rain by rights was snow for cold.
The wind was another layer of mould.
But the strangest thing: in the thick old thatch,
Where summer birds had been given hatch,
Had fed in chorus, and lived to fledge,
Some still were living in hermitage.
And as I passed along the eaves,
So low I brushed the straw with my sleeves,
I flushed birds out of hole after hole,
Into the darkness. It grieved my soul,
It started a grief within a grief,
To think their case was beyond relief –
They could not go flying about in search
Of their nest again, nor find a perch.
They must brood where they fell in mulch and mire,
Trusting feathers and inward fire
Till daylight made it safe for a flyer.
My greater grief was by so much reduced
As I thought of them without nest or roost.
That was how that grief started to melt.
They tell me the cottage where we dwelt,
Its wind-torn thatch goes now unmended;
Its life of hundreds of years has ended
By letting the rain I knew outdoors
In on to the upper chamber floors.

Abercrombie wrote passionately in 'Ryton Firs' of the trees near Gallows Cottage, and it was for him that Frost wrote 'The Sound of the Trees', inspired however, by the trees on a hill some way beyond The Gallows. According to John Haines, Frost had told him that he also had in mind a group of trees near his old home in New England.

Robert Frost

THE SOUND OF THE TREES

I wonder about the trees.
Why do we wish to bear
Forever the noise of these
More than another noise
So close to our dwelling place?
We suffer them by the day
Till we lose all measure of pace,
And fixity in our joys,
And acquire a listening air.
They are that that talks of going
But never gets away;
And that talks no less for knowing,
As it grows wiser and older,
That now it means to stay.
My feet tug at the floor
And my head sways to my shoulder
Sometimes when I watch trees sway,
From the window or the door.
I shall set forth for somewhere,
I shall make the reckless choice
Some day when they are in voice
And tossing so as to scare
The white clouds over them on.
I shall have less to say,
But I shall be gone.

Frost, perhaps mindful of his place as an American poet, could never be pinned down about the influence of his stay in Dymock on his poetry, but Haines tells us that Frost wrote many of the poems in *Mountain Interval* at Leddington and Ryton, and remembers him reading several of them to him in Gloucestershire, including 'The Sound of the Trees', 'The Hyla Brook', 'The Exposed Nest' and 'Birches'.

BIRCHES

When I see birches bend to left and right
Across the lines of straighter darker trees,
I like to think some boy's been swinging them.
But swinging doesn't bend them down to stay
As ice-storms do. Often you must have seen them
Loaded with ice a sunny winter morning
After a rain. They click upon themselves
As the breeze rises, and turn many-coloured

73

As the stir cracks and crazes their enamel.
Soon the sun's warmth makes them shed crystal shells
Shattering and avalanching on the snow-crust –
Such heaps of broken glass to sweep away
You'd think the inner dome of heaven had fallen.
They are dragged to the withered bracken by the load,
And they seem not to break; though once they are bowed
So low for long, they never right themselves:
You may see their trunks arching in the woods
Years afterwards, trailing their leaves on the ground
Like girls on hands and knees that throw their hair
Before them over their heads to dry in the sun.
But I was going to say when Truth broke in
With all her matter-of-fact about the ice-storm
I should prefer to have some boy bend them
As he went out and in to fetch the cows –
Some boy too far from town to learn baseball,
Whose only play was what he found himself,
Summer or winter, and could play alone.
One by one he subdued his father's trees
By riding them down over and over again
Until he took the stiffness out of them,
And not one but hung limp, not one was left
For him to conquer. He learned all there was
To learn about not launching out too soon
And so not carrying the tree away
Clear to the ground. He always kept his poise
To the top branches, climbing carefully
With the same pains you use to fill a cup
Up to the brim, and even above the brim.
Then he flung outward, feet first, with a swish,
Kicking his way down through the air to the ground.
So was I once myself a swinger of birches.
And so I dream of going back to be.
It's when I'm weary of considerations,
And life is too much like a pathless wood
Where your face burns and tickles with the cobwebs
Broken across it, and one eye is weeping
From a twig's having lashed across it open.
I'd like to get away from earth awhile
And then come back to it and begin over.
May no fate wilfully misunderstand me
And half grant what I wish and snatch me away
Not to return. Earth's the right place for love:
I don't know where it's likely to go better.
I'd like to go by climbing a birch tree,
And climb black branches up a snow-white trunk

> *Toward* heaven, till the tree could bear no more,
> But dipped its top and set me down again.
> That would be good both going and coming back.
> One could do worse than be a swinger of birches.

The Frosts eventually returned to America, sailing from Liverpool on February 13th, 1915. Robert Frost never forgot his time with his poet friends in Dymock and twice came back to Britain to visit. He maintained a regular correspondence with the people he had met in Britain, especially Abercrombie, to whom he wrote in 1925:

> I cling more than I can tell you to your friendship in poetry. Yours was the first praise over there and there will never be any other just like it . . . Now I should like to go out into the yard and shake hands with your big cold pump till his iron tank was as full of water as my heart is of Ryton memories.

NOTES

1 Louis Mertins, *Robert Frost: Life and Talks-Walking*, (University of Oklahoma Press, 1965).
2 Edward Thomas's *In Pursuit of Spring*, published earlier that year by Thomas Nelson.
3 Louis Mertins, ibid.
4 Eleanor Farjeon, *Edward Thomas: The Last Four Years*, (Oxford University Press, 1979).
5 Helen Thomas, *Time & Again*, (new ed. Carcanet Press, 1978).
6 Letter, Robert Frost to John Haines, July 1914.
7 John Haines, 'Mr Robert Frost: an American Poet in Gloucestershire', *Gloucester Journal*, February 2nd, 1935.
8 Louis Mertins, ibid.
9 Letter, Robert Frost to Sidney Cox, September 17th, 1914.

Edward Thomas

For Edward Thomas it was not so much the attraction of the Gloucestershire countryside that drew him to Dymock in 1914 but the opportunity to continue the friendship that had begun the previous year in London with Robert Frost. It was a friendship that was to have a profound effect on both their lives.

They first met in February, 1913 at the East Grinstead home of poet and antique dealer Vivian Locke Ellis, where Thomas rented a study to write away from domestic problems and to be nearer to London's publishers, agents and magazine editors. Frost and Thomas met again in the autumn of that year, through Ralph Hodgson at a vegetarian restaurant, St George's, in St Martin's Lane, London. The unpretentious third floor room, reached by a small side door to the right of the restaurant entrance, up two flights of brass-lined stairs and through a door marked 'Smoking', had become one of a number of regular lunchtime rendezvous for London's literary talent. Thomas also attended a lunchtime club above the Mont Blanc Restaurant in Gerrard Street, Soho, where Edward Garnett, an influential figure in the publishing world and a close friend of Thomas's, held court every Tuesday and Wednesday.

Edward Thomas made weekly visits to the capital to sell review books, a necessary way of supplementing his income, and had become such a regular at the St George's that his poet friends nicknamed him 'The Iambic'. Here he met some of the day's rising stars, many of whose work he had known and reviewed, including Arthur Ransome and W.H. Davies, whom he had befriended and provided with a study (at a time when he could least afford to do so). It was Thomas who raised the money when Davies needed a new wooden leg and who helped find a publisher for his *Autobiography of a Supertramp* as well as acting in an editorial capacity. Some years later their roles were reversed and it was Davies who contacted his literary friends to see if help could be found to ease Thomas's financial problems.

It was at Thomas's request that Hodgson introduced Frost on October 4th, 1913. They met again two days later, Thomas cancelling a pre-arranged visit to see Eleanor Farjeon. Throughout the following months the two men met regularly. Roughly the same age, Frost and Thomas had much in common, not just their literary interests but on a personal level too. It wasn't that they came from similar backgrounds, far from it, but Frost had suffered problems in his life that Thomas was still experiencing, and was able to help him in his struggles.

Edward Thomas

Born in south London in 1878, the son of a Welsh civil servant with the railways, Thomas had one desire from an early age: to write, a craving fuelled by the discovery of nature writers like Richard Jefferies. Thomas and his father were to become almost completely alienated, the father never understanding the son's ambitions to write. Their lack of warmth to each other, from which Thomas suffered throughout his life, is more than obviously shown in the rather bitter poem 'P.H.T.' written towards the end of 1915 on seeing his father in town a few weeks earlier when they had argued about the war. The poet found his father's contempt hurtful. "He treats me so that I have a feeling of shame that I am alive" he wrote to Frost.

The craving to write, combined with the need to support a family (he had married Helen Noble, the daughter of James Ashcroft Noble, the critic and writer, in 1899) had an even worse effect on Thomas than the bad relationship with his father. He became an essayist, a prolific and highly influential literary critic and the writer of 'pot-boilers'. This brought on, or at least encouraged, deep depressions, fits of anger, a self-torturing sense of failure and even suicidal moods. Frost suffered similar problems and was able to help Thomas, if not cure his 'black melancholia', at least to come to terms with it. It was not just Frost's counselling, but as much the discovery that he could write poetry that brought Thomas relief and satisfaction. Strangely enough army life, after he had enlisted in 1915, lessened the pressure on Thomas and allowed him to write for the first time without financial worries.

In the spring of 1914, Thomas and his son Merfyn travelled to Beaconsfield from their home in Petersfield and stayed with the Frosts, who were then preparing for the move to Gloucestershire. Thomas also stayed with them at Little Iddens on three occasions before he took rooms for his family's long August stay at the Leddington farmhouse of Mr and Mrs Chandler. The first visit to Little Iddens was made in April, very soon after the Frosts had moved. Thomas, son and eldest daughter Bronwen, stayed on their return from a cycling trip to Wales.

That Thomas was one of the welcomed guests is evident from a letter Elinor Frost wrote to her sister Leona after the critic had made that first visit to Little Iddens: "Rob and I think everything of him. He was quite the most admirable and loveable man we have every known." It was an opinion shared it seems by almost every person who came into contact with the charismatic Thomas. Gordon Bottomley, his old friend in the Lake District, wrote in 1908:

Edward Thomas

TO EDWARD THOMAS

Here in the North we speak of you,
And dream (and wish the dream were true)
That when the evening has grown late
You will appear outside our gate –
As though some Gipsy-Scholar yet
Sought this far place that men forget;
Or some tall hero still unknown
Out of the Mabinogion,
Were seen at nightfall looking in,
Passing mysteriously to win
His earlier earth, his ancient mind,
Where man was true and life more kind
Lived with the mountains and the trees
And other steadfast presences,
Where large and simple passions gave
The insight and the peace we crave,
And he no more had nigh forgot
The old high battles he had fought.

Because your heart could understand
The hopes of their primeval land,
The hearts of dim heroic forms
Made clear by tenderness and storms
You caught my glow and urged me on;
So now the tale is once more done
I bring my play, I turn to you
And wish it might to-night be true
That you would seek this old small house
Twixt laurel boughs and apple boughs;
Then I would give it, bravely manned,
To you, and with my play my hand.

Edward Thomas loved the simple things of life: flowers, fishing, gardening, drying herbs and making furniture. Children loved him, so did dogs. He was always the same whether he was talking to a local villager or a famous writer. His self-torment, though, showed itself in a sad expression and an inhibiting shyness and self-consciousness that could be mistaken for coldness or even superiority. When Edward Garnett tried to make Thomas aware of this disadvantage – especially when approaching publishers – Thomas replied with the poem 'I Built Myself a House of Glass'.

Helen Thomas and their youngest daughter Myfanwy did not make the trip to Little Iddens on this first visit, remaining at their Petersfield home to look after holiday boarders from nearby Bedales, a co-educational school with a strong emphasis on the arts and crafts.

Thomas's second visit took place on June 16th, 1914 when he spent three days there, breaking the return journey from a visit to the Lake District to see the invalided poet Gordon Bottomley. On the journey to Gloucester on June 23rd, the train made an unscheduled stop at the Gloucestershire village of Adlestrop, which he recorded in his note book "Then we stopped at Adlestrop, through the willows could be heard a chain of blackbirds' songs at 12.45 and one thrush and no man seen, only a hiss of engine letting off steam."[1] The result was one of Thomas's most popular poems with its remarkable, memorable opening line.

ADLESTROP

Yes, I remember Adlestrop –
The name, because one afternoon
Of heat the express-train drew up there
Unwontedly. It was late June.

The steam hissed. Someone cleared his throat.
No one left and no one came
On the bare platform. What I saw
was Adlestrop – only the name.

And willows, willow-herb, and grass
And meadow-sweet, and haycocks dry,
No whit less still and lonely fair
Than the high cloudlets in the sky.

And for that minute a blackbird sang
Close by, and round him, mistier,
Farther and farther, all the birds
Of Oxfordshire and Gloucestershire.

Thomas remembered Adlestrop in verse – and Adlestrop remembered him, though perhaps in a less than prestigious way, for the poem is to be found inscribed on a plaque fixed to a bench in the village bus shelter. Adlestrop is a quiet village of mellow Cotswold stone in the Evenlode Valley. Jane Austen had visited it over a century earlier, when her uncle was the local rector and a considerable landowner. The station where Thomas's train made its stop stood close to the River Evenlode and about a mile from the village. There is no station today, through express trains still travel the line between Oxford and Worcester, though without a hint of hissing steam. The name board that Thomas saw on the station and the platform bench, in their Great Western

Railway brown and cream livery, now in the village bus shelter, are all that remain of the station, made famous when a train made an 'unwonted' stop one hot June day.

It was during this June visit that Frost took Thomas to meet the Abercrombies and, at the home of Wilfrid Gibson, Thomas renewed his friendship with Rupert Brooke, recently returned from his lengthy tour. Brooke and Thomas had known each other for some years, when Brooke had been at Cambridge and fallen in love with a young girl who was a pupil at Bedales. Forbidden by her sisters to see her, Brooke resorted to subterfuge, to arrange 'accidental' meetings, and Thomas was drawn in to help. On one occasion, the girl was invited by the Thomases to their home for tea when one of the other guests happened to be Rupert Brooke. The critic also visited Brooke, in October 1913, at his home in Grantchester, and shortly afterwards Brooke stayed with Thomas.

Despite the closeness of Thomas to Frost, Helen Thomas did not meet him until July, when she accompanied her husband to Little Iddens for the first time and saw the relationship that had grown between the two men: "It was at once obvious that Robert and Edward were very congenial to each other."[2] A few weeks later, the Thomases came to Gloucestershire to spend the whole month of August near the Frosts, renting rooms at the farmhouse, Oldfields, a short walk from Little Iddens, for three guineas a week.

They travelled in two separate parties. Thomas and Merfyn cycled there while the rest of the family stayed at home an extra day so that the third child, Myfanwy, could be treated for her weak eyesight.

The cyclists set out on August 3rd on a route that let Thomas visit an old friend, Jesse Berridge, at Swindon, and point out to his son many of the places he remembered when he visited relatives in Wiltshire as a youth and where an old countryman, David Uzzell, had become more of a father to him than his natural parent. Edward Thomas was excited by the trip, writing to Eleanor Farjeon the day before they set out:

> . . . it is no use trying to write. I think only about Alton Basingstoke Newbury Hungerford Aldborne Swindon Cricklade Cirencester Gloucester Ledbury all the time . . .[3]

For Helen, daughters Bronwen and Myfanwy, the pet dog Rags and a Russian boy Peter Mrosovski, a pupil at Bedales who was boarding with them, the trip to Dymock was harrowing. They left on a blazing hot Bank Holiday Sunday, August 4th, the day the newspapers announced that Britain had issued her ultimatum to the German Government to guarantee Belgium's neutrality. It would have been a long and difficult journey at the best of times; in the face of the news it became a traumatic one. Helen Thomas later wrote of the journey at length in *Time & Again*.[4]

> I forget if there was any unusual crowd of passengers on Petersfield station, but as we proceeded on our journey it was obvious from the crowds in the stations we stopped at that people were in a state of excitement. Families on holiday were hurrying home, reservists were being called up and soldiers recalled from leave, and everywhere the stations were thronged with trunks, kitbags and other luggage and with restless and anxious people. However, very much later than our scheduled time we reached Oxford. Here we were told to leave the train which, in the ordinary way would have gone on to complete our journey. The station was in a state of chaos.

After a long wait, a train arrived which took them on a slow journey, with many stops between stations, to Malvern. They arrived at midnight. There would be no more trains that night, they were told, and they could not sleep in the station waiting room. So the Thomas party, bags and dogs, climbed into a taxi to complete the journey.

> The country was entirely unknown to me, and I had not the least idea, as we drove off uphill in the darkness, how far away we were from our destination or in what direction it lay. But I shall never forget that drive over the Malvern Hills which a huge full harvest moon lighted up like a stage set. Even in my distress and weariness I was entranced by the beauty of the scene and the silence and mystery of the deserted countryside, either in deepest shadow or brilliant moonlight.[5]

In the market square at Ledbury the taxi driver stopped and asked the way from a policeman. Who were his travellers and where were they going at this time of night? That one of the party was Russian made the policeman even more suspicious and when Helen Thomas mentioned that they were friends of Robert Frost, in the hopes that his name might be familiar to the officer, it only made things worse. Frost was already under suspicion, being a foreigner. The policeman eventually gave directions to Leddington and Oldfields, where Edward Thomas was waiting for them at the gate.

The Thomases had not been at Leddington for many days when the village policeman called to tell them that several anonymous letters had been received at headquarters, in addition to the report from the policeman the party had met on their way, suggesting that there were spies amongst the newcomers: "Evidently, we thought, the result of our midnight interview with the policeman at Ledbury, or the villagers' suspicion of us as strangers who sat up very late at night in the Frosts' isolated cottage, and whose unconventional ways they could not understand."[6] Edward Thomas saw the funny side of it, but Frost could not, and later threatened he would shoot the policeman if he ever came "nosing about here again". Frost's temper and irritation were illustrated during Thomas's 1915 visit to The Gallows, where the Frosts were staying with the Abercrombies. An aged gamekeeper, 'Ole Bott' at Gamage Hall near Ryton pulled a shotgun on Frost and Thomas during one of their walks. According to some sources the gamekeeper mistrusted them because of the talk of spies, but more likely because they were on private land belonging to Lord Beauchamp. The gamekeeper had a reputation for being over-zealous.

The walkers retreated, but Frost grew increasingly angry and persuaded Thomas to return with him to the keeper's cottage where he threatened him in no uncertain terms. That evening the village policeman visited Frost with orders to arrest him, but instead told him that, knowing the gamekeeper and his bullying ways, he had no intention of doing so. Lord Beauchamp heard of the incident and, realising the social standing of these literary newcomers, rebuked the gamekeeper, apologised to Frost and arranged that, like Gibson and Abercrombie, he should have free access to his lands. This was to become one of Frost's favourite stories and, like all good tales, became more elaborate with retelling. Was the incident in Thomas's mind when he wrote the fourth verse of his Lincolnshire Poacher-inspired 'An Old Song'?

AN OLD SONG

I was not apprenticed nor ever dwelt in famous Lincolnshire,
I've served one master ill and well much more than seven year;
And never took up to poaching as you shall quickly find;
But 'tis my delight of a shiny night in the season of the year.

I roamed where nobody had a right but keepers and squires, and there
I sought for nests, wild flowers, oak sticks, and moles, both far and near.
And had to run from farmers, and learnt the Lincolnshire song:
'Oh, 'tis my delight of a shiny night in the season of the year.'

I took those walks years after, talking with friend or dear,
Or solitary musing, but when the moon shone clear
I had no joy or sorrow that could not be expressed
By 'Tis my delight of a shiny night in the season of the year.'

Since then I've thrown away a chance to fight a gamekeeper;
And I less often trespass, and what I see or hear
Is mostly from the road or path by day; yet still I sing:
'Oh, 'tis my delight of a shiny night in the season of the year.'

For if I am contented, at home or anywhere,
Or if I sigh for I know not what, or my heart beats with some fear,
It is a strange kind of delight to sing or whistle just:
'Oh, 'tis my delight of a shiny night in the season of the year.'

And with this melody on my lips and no one by to care,
Indoors, or out on shiny nights or dark in open air,
I am for a moment made a man that sings out of his heart:
'Oh, 'tis my delight of a shiny night in the season of the year.'

Thomas, who often entertained the Frosts in the evenings at Little Iddens with his fine singing voice, had a large repertoire of English folk songs (many of them bawdy) and, the song 'I'll go no more a-roving with you fair maid' provided the inspiration for another poem, which he also entitled 'An Old Song'.

For all his depressions, Edward Thomas enjoyed good company, especially when it was with people whose talent he respected, and the weeks that followed must have seemed almost perfect. There were, however, bad days when his melancholia returned: he must have been suffering from a depression the day he wrote from Leddington to Eleanor Farjeon:

> We are doing rather moderately here. The boys are bored. Peter is here – he helps raise the standard of what boys may do, I suppose . . . Helen is not up to much, and I don't help. One thing and another leaves me very irritable indeed. The quarters are too close . . . Baby is grizzling upstairs. The Frosts are all over the house seeing Mr Chandler off. Peter's chair creaks as he reads the Baroness Orczy and Mervyn sounds incompletely satisfied with the old *Strand* magazine. But it is a very fine hot day. God is in *His* heaven all right, obviously and ostentatiously. Mr Chandler will be in *his* in Hereford.[7]

Mr Chandler, who farmed Oldfields, was a reservist and had already been called up to rejoin his regiment.

Despite the tone of this letter, Thomas and Frost were by choice rarely out of each other's company, and daily Thomas would walk over to Little Iddens, crossing the three meadows sometimes as often as three times a day:

> The first was a concave meadow, in April strewn with daffodils. There, day and night, pastured a bay colt and a black mare, thirty years old, but gay enough to have slipped away two years back and got herself made the mother of this 'stolen' foal. The path led across the middle of the meadow, through a gate, and alongside one of the hedges of the next, which sloped down rather steeply to the remnant of brook, and was grazed by half a dozen cows. At the bottom a hedge followed the line of the brook and a stile took me through it, with a deep drop, to a plank and a puddle, and so to the last field, a rough one. This rose up as steeply and was the night's lodging of four cart horses. The path, having gradually approached a hedge on the left, went alongside it, under the horse-chestnut tree leaning out of it, and in sight of the house, until it reached the far hedge and the road . . . How easy it was to spend a morning or afternoon in walking over to this house, stopping to talk to whoever was about for a few minutes . . .[8]

The two families met together beneath the open beams of Little Iddens to talk and sing folk songs, to drink cider and locally made perry, sit in the orchards and fields to play with the children. They walked the footpaths, they explored the woods and studied the wild flowers in this beautiful countryside:

> It was mostly orchard and grass, gently up and down, seldom steep for more than a few yards. Some of the meadows had a group or a line of elms; one an ash rising out of an islet of dense brambles; many had several great old apple or pear trees. The pears were small brown perry pears, as thick as haws, the apples chiefly cider apples, innumerable, rosy and uneatable, though once or twice we did pick up a wasp's remnant, with slightly greasy skin of palest yellow, that tasted delicious. There was one brook to cross, shallow and leaden, with high hollow bare banks. More than one meadow was trenched, apparently by a dried watercourse, showing flags, rushes, and a train of willows.[9]

One day the Thomases and the Frosts joined forces to dig the potato patch at Little Iddens, as Eleanor Farjeon, who had by then joined them, renting rooms at a neighbouring house, recalled:

> In the morning we all turned up on the Frost' 'lot' with potato forks; the rows were divided among us . . . The only indolent member of the outfit was Robert, who, smoking blandly, strolled up and down the patch, a self-appointed overseer of cheap labour; while with sleeves rolled up and sweat pouring down we forked our allotted rows. We stopped only for cups of tea in a corner of the ground, and, as we finished, one by one we downed forks. The mounds of earthy spuds lay exposed among the fallen haulms like a gold-digger's nuggets encrusted with quartz.[10]

Farjeon remembered at one point a triangle of ground still lay undug and Thomas jokingly pointed to it and said to his 'overseer' "Wot abaht that little bit, mister?"

> That blazing afternoon turning to twilight in the potato-field, with the welcome drinks, the bodily toil and ease of spirit, and Edward playing labourer to Robert's boss, is a memory that quickens whenever I recall it. The pleasure sprang from Edward's relaxation in Robert's company. The humour of the two friends was in perfect accord . . .[11]

After supper, the toilers gathered in the small living room of Little Iddens, most of them sitting on the floor, where the discussion inevitably turned to the one subject that was to dominate every meeting between the two men: the nature of poetry.

The weeks at Leddington turned Edward Thomas's life and career upside down. He had already made his name as a literary critic, admired for his erudition and his knowledge of poetry. He had also written numerous biographies, collections of essays, articles and books of his walks through the English and Welsh countryside. At Dymock he realised his vocation as a poet. It was not a sudden transformation, of course, for Thomas had been re-examining his writing for some time. He had been trying to shake off the influence of Pater and others whose elegant and grandiose prose, carefully wrought and honed down to its most 'perfect' form, had produced a style of writing where the words seemed to have more importance than the content. He had been turning more and more to the influences of his earlier days, like Richard Jefferies whose writing had so excited him in his boyhood days in South London where the 'country' was the commonland at Clapham and Wandsworth. There is a perceptible move in the later books, especially the fictional *The Happy-Go-Lucky-Morgans* and *In Pursuit of Spring*, towards a much freer style, a loosening and a simplification, a style more akin to the way people spoke in real life.

It can only be conjectured whether Thomas would have discovered his latent talent anyway, but at Dymock Frost proved the catalyst that speeded up the process. The American shared many of his views about poetry and the need to free the spoken language, as he had shown in *North of Boston* which Thomas reviewed extremely favourably on two occasions; in one extensive review for *The Daily News* he called it ". . . one of the most revolutionary books of modern times, but one of the quietest and least aggressive".

> These poems are revolutionary because they lack the exaggeration of rhetoric, and even at first sight appear to lack the poetic intensity of which rhetoric is an imitation. Their language is free from the poetic words and forms that are the chief material of secondary poets. The metre avoids not only the old-fashioned pomp and sweetness, but the later fashion also of discord and fuss. In fact the medium is common speech and common decasyllables . . .

And in *New Weekly* of August 8th, 1914, Thomas gives an admirable description of Frost's style and his use of common plain speech:

> Mr Frost has, in fact, gone back, as Whitman and as Wordsworth went back, through the paraphernalia of poetry into poetry again. With a confidence like genius, he has trusted his convictions that a man will not easily write better than he speaks when some matter has touched him deeply and when he has turned it over until he has no doubt what it means to him, when he has no purpose to serve beyond expressing it, when he has no audience to be bullied or flattered, when he is free, and speech takes one form and no other.

The great debate between Frost and Thomas over this shared philosophy dominated the hot summer of 1914 as the two writers walked the countryside of Gloucestershire and Herefordshire:

Edward Thomas

THE SUN USED TO SHINE

The sun used to shine while we two walked
Slowly together, paused and started
Again, and sometimes mused, sometimes talked
As either pleased, and cheerfully parted.

Each night. We never disagreed
Which gate to rest on. The to be
And the late past we gave small heed.
We turned from men or poetry

To rumours of the war remote
Only till both stood disinclined
For aught but the yellow flavorous coat
Of an apple wasps had undermined;

Or a sentry of dark betonies,
The stateliest of small flowers on earth,
At the forest verge; or crocuses
Pale purple as if they had their birth

In sunless Hades fields. The war
Came back to mind with the moonrise
Which soldiers in the east afar
Beheld then. Nevertheless, our eyes

Could as well imagine the Crusades
Or Caesar's battles. Everything
To faintness like those rumours fades –
Like the brook's water glittering

Under the moonlight – like those walks
Now – like us two that took them, and
The fallen apples, all the talks
And silences – like the memory's sand

When the tide covers it late or soon
And other men through other flowers
In those fields under the same moon
Go talking and have easy hours.

If talk dwindled in the traversing of a big field, the pause at gate or stile braced it again. Often we prolonged the pause, whether we actually sat or not, and we talked – of flowers, childhood, Shakespeare, women, England, the war – or we looked at a far horizon, which some dip or gap occasionally disclosed.[12]

Eleanor Farjeon recounted how on one walk Frost was talking of what he called the 'cadence' in the human voice which accompanied the speech that came naturally to it, and in the fields of Dymock found an example to illustrate his point.

> While we walked, we saw across two hedgerows a man's figure standing against the skyline on top of a cart; he had a fork in his hands with which he caught and attacked some load, corn or manure, pitched from below. Frost stopped and shouted a question across the fields – it might have been, 'What are you doing there, this fine afternoon?' but whatever the words the man could not have heard them. He too shouted some answer that rang through the air, and it was impossible for us to distinguish what he said but the cadence of the answer was as clear as that of the question. Robert turned to Edward, 'That's what I mean,' he said.[13]

These discussions, his regard for Frost's intellect and talent, and Frost's recognition of the poetic nature of his prose led to what Farjeon called the 'undamming' of Edward Thomas. He almost forsook all forms of prose from that time. During the next three years he wrote some 170 poems which have become recognised as amongst the best of his generation, eclipsing the work of many of the poets he reviewed so favourably in the press and outshining those poets who had seen him as a 'faded writer'. The satisfaction he received in verse was something he had never found in his prose and this, and the freedom from having to write to order to support his family that enlisting in the army had brought, transformed the moody Thomas in his final years before he died in action in 1917.

Frost was always at pains to deprecate his part in the dramatic change in Thomas's life that occured after Dymock. Writing to the American poet Grace Walcott Corkling in 1921, Frost explained that all he did was show Thomas that he had been a poet all his life but hadn't recognised it in himself.

> I dragged him out from under the heap of his own work in prose he was buried alive under. He was throwing to his big perfunctory histories of Marlborough and the like written to order such poetry as would make him a name if he were but given credit for it. I made him see that he owed it to himself and to poetry to have it out by itself in poetic form where it must suffer itself to be admired. It took me some time. I bantered, teased and bullied all the summer we were together at Leddington and Ryton . . . It was plain that he had wanted to be a poet all the years he had been writing about poets not worth his little finger. But he was afeared . . .

He ended: "The point is that what we had in common we had from before we were born."

On another occasion, Frost wrote: "Right at that moment he was writing as good poetry as anyone alive, but in prose form where it did not declare itself and gain him recognition. I referred him to paragraphs in his book *In Pursuit of Spring* and told him to write it in verse form in exactly the same cadence." Despite Frost's modesty, he was undoubtedly the prime cause of Thomas's 'undamming'. It was a process that had begun in the spring of 1914. On May 19th, 1914 Thomas wrote to the American: "I wonder whether you can imagine me taking to verse. If you can I might get over feeling it is impossible – which at once obliges your good nature to say 'I can'." Helen Thomas recognised Frost's vital role in *World Without End* in which she changed the names of the main characters, with her husband becoming 'David':

> Between him and David a most wonderful friendship grew up. He believed in David and loved him, understanding, as no other man had ever understood, his strange complex temperament. The influence of this man on David's intellectual life was profound, and to it alone of outside influences is to be attributed that final and fullest expression of himself which David now found in writing poetry.[14]

Frost of course was not the only person to recognise the poetic quality of Thomas's prose. W.H. Hudson wrote about the recently published fictional *The Happy-Go-Lucky-Morgans* to Edward Garnett: ". . . I believe he has taken the wrong path and is wandering lost in the vast wilderness . . . He is essentially a poet . . ."[15] Eleanor Farjeon, after reading Thomas's *Light and Twilight* asked the author if he had ever written poetry, to which he replied "Me? I couldn't write a poem to save my life," but in a letter to her on August 2nd, 1914, just before he set off for Dymock, he wrote, referring to his latest manuscript *Homes and Haunts* and its fate in the light of an impending war: "Who will want the thing now? I may as well write poetry. Did anyone ever begin at 36 in the shade?"

Yet, a few weeks later, with Frost's encouragement still ringing in his ears, Thomas, with some temerity, did turn to writing poetry. His earliest works appeared in anthologies under a pseudonym, Edward Eastaway. That here was a new poet of considerable substance was soon apparent to the reviewers, who singled out his work in the anthologies for special mention ahead of poets a great deal more established. Solomon Eagle (J.C. Squire) in his review of *An Annual of New Poetry* made disparaging remarks about Gibson, Drinkwater and Frost but had nothing but praise for 'Edward Eastaway', the real identity of whom the reviewer stated he was aware:

One's knowledge did not preposses one in favour of his poetry; one did not think that a real gift of verse could remain so long unexploited without being atrophied. But the unlikely has happened; and his poems are better than his prose, good though some of this has been. There are not enough of them here to give an exact notion of his power and his limitations. But 'The Wood', 'Aspens', 'The Brook', 'Wind and Mist' and 'For These' would, by themselves, be enough to show that he is worth fifty Frosts . . .[16]

NOTES

1 Field Note Book No.75. Edward Thomas kept copious notes for use in books and articles in what are called his Field Note Books. These are now in the Berg Collection in New York Public Library.
2 Helen Thomas, 'Poets' Holiday in the Shadow of War', *The Times*, August 3rd, 1963.
3 Letter, Edward Thomas to Eleanor Farjeon, August 2nd, 1914.
4 Helen Thomas, *Time & Again*, (Carcanet Press, 1978).
5 Helen Thomas, *Time & Again*, ibid.
6 Helen Thomas, *Time & Again*, ibid.
7 Letter, Edward Thomas to Eleanor Farjeon, August 14th, 1914 in Eleanor Farjeon, *Edward Thomas: The Last Four Years*, (Oxford University Press, 1979).
8 Edward Thomas, 'This England', *The Nation*, November 7th, 1914.
9 Edward Thomas, ibid.
10 Eleanor Farjeon, ibid.
11 Eleanor Farjeon, ibid.
12 Edward Thomas, ibid.
13 Eleanor Farjeon, ibid.
14 Helen Thomas, *World Without End*, (Heinemann, 1931). In *Under Storm's Wing* (Carcanet Press, 1988) a general compilation of Helen Thomas' evocative autobiographical text, the real names have been used in *World Without End*.
15 Letters from W.H. Hudson to Edward Garnett, London 1925.
16 *New Statesman*, March 31st, 1917.

Eleanor Farjeon

As Thomas had come to Gloucestershire to continue a growing friendship with Frost, so Eleanor Farjeon came in August 1914 to be with Thomas. For her, it was not for comradeship with a like-minded person but for love, a fact recognised by Thomas (though she never proclaimed her feelings to him) but not returned. He did, however, regard her as a dear friend and confidante – and, when he was in uniform, as his unpaid secretary, the typist of his poetry and his manuscripts. They had met when he had been staying at the home of Clifford Bax and she and her brother Bertie, were among the other guests, as was Rupert Brooke. Helen Thomas was aware of the young girl's feelings towards her husband, but, realising that her friendship was good for him, encouraged her to become close to the family. Indeed, the two women, though so very different, admired and respected each other's qualities and became intimate friends. Helen Thomas described Eleanor Farjeon as witty, a vivacious talker, extremely entertaining, with a quick intelligence and great vitality. Farjeon, who once reassured Helen Thomas that even though she loved her husband she would do nothing to threaten their marriage, also became a 'favourite aunt' to the Thomas children who greatly loved her and found her a perfect companion.

In July, 1914 Eleanor Farjeon had gone to the family holiday-place at Overstrand in Norfolk, but had come back to London early, having found the bracing Norfolk sea air disagreeable. The Thomases suggested that, if they could find suitable lodgings for her, she should join them in Gloucestershire and meet Frost, whose *North of Boston* she had read and admired. She could not leave London immediately because her mother was not well, so it was arranged that she should come to Leddington later in August.

On August 20th she travelled to Leddington where the Thomases had fixed rooms for her at Glyn Iddens, just behind the Frosts' cottage and a short walk across the fields from their own accommodation at Oldfields. Her hosts were Mr Farmer, an elderly countryman 'with bad teeth and an easy manner' and his large, domineering wife, very much, says Farjeon, the 'Captain of the ship'. Her accommodation, for which she paid £1 a week, comprised a living room and a bedroom above it, large square rooms with windows facing the lane. She was provided with three large meals a day, eaten in the Farmers' dining room, with its old-fashioned fireplace and vast sideboard. The bedroom had a huge double bed, with a 'mountainous' feather mattress stuffed by Mrs Farmer using feathers from her own geese. "It was so heavy that I could not have lugged it off the bed, but in the mornings Mrs Farmer tossed it like a pancake, trounching and pummelling it as though she was kneading a gigantic mass of dough . . ."[1] In the cellars, the Farmers kept their home-brewed cider; they seem to have disapproved of water as a drink, and a pewter jug of cider was kept filled on the sideboard. Around the house were the orchards where they cultivated plums, pears, gages, nectarines and dessert apples for the London market – the high quality fruit that Carol Frost was allowed to help pick – as well as cider apples for their own pressing. They also kept some livestock: chickens, geese and pigs for home-cured bacon.

Eleanor Farjeon's stay here was short but she approached it with customary vitality. She was a great walker and loved the countryside around Dymock, though as ignorant as Frost of the names of the wild flowers she saw. Young Bronwen Thomas, aged ten, was 'shocked' at her ignorance and set out to teach her about the flowers that grew so abundantly here, setting her exam papers to test whether she had learned everything she had been taught. Eleanor Farjeon typically entered whole-heartedly into the spirit of it and proved to be a 'model pupil'.

She had not met Robert Frost before this holiday, nor had she met Abercrombie or Gibson; indeed she never met them again after it. There was one evening when the whole of the 'resident' muse colony – the Abercrombies, Frosts, Gibsons and Thomases – dined at Glyn Iddens, at the invitation of Mrs Farmer. This meal was very amusingly described in full in her memoir of Edward Thomas:

> Literary fame was in the air, and the ebbs and flow of poets suddenly went to Mrs Farmer's head. One morning she presented herself with a request. Did I think, she asked with great dignity, that it would be in order for her to invite Mr and Mrs Thomas and Mr and Mrs Frost to supper one evening? I was sure they would be delighted. Then, would I undertake to ask them for next Sunday? I would, with pleasure. Did I think it would be the proper thing to ask Mr Gibson and Mr Abercrombie too? I undertook these invitations too.

Eleanor ran down to the Thomases and then to the Frosts to deliver the invitations and warn them to come in their best clothes, as this was to be "an Occasion" and by the next day Mrs Farmer had received acceptances from her literary guests. When the day arrived Eleanor spent it among the Frost and Thomas children, went home to change but when she came downstairs the entrance to the dining room was barred by Mrs Farmer, dressed in her best black dress and an apron.

> 'The Guests will be sitting in the parlour before supper, Miss Farjeon, and as I shall be busy in the kitchen will you be so kind as to entertain them for me?' So

saying, she opened the door into the closed room; the double doors between it and the dining-room were still sealed. The back room was almost too good to be true; it was the stage-producer's dream of any middle-class Best Parlour in any Victorian play. It was crowded with more old-fashioned furniture than could be taken in by the late summer light which scarcely penetrated the shrubs against the windows, and the table-lamps which diffused yellow pools only on the objects that surrounded them on the plush covers. There was a scroll-back sofa and arm-chairs to match, and some uncompromising chairs; the mantlepiece ornaments and the pictures on the walls could not have been other than they were. The room smelt musty, but it was not dusty; Mrs Farmer's massive arms had been at work.'

Mrs Farmer showed Eleanor various books in the room, photograph albums that 'The Guests' might look at while they waited. The first to arrive were the Frosts and the Thomases who were shown into the back-room by Mrs Farmer. Following her host's wishes, Eleanor gravely greeted them and provided each with a Family Album while Mrs Farmer retired back to the kitchen. The poets and their wives had indeed put on their best clothes and the influence of this and the parlour seems to have overcome their usual exuberance and talkativeness – they talked politely in hushed voices leafing through the albums. Gibson and Abercrombie then arrived and were each given their family album to peruse. "I think we all felt bound by an unspoken conspiracy not to let our hosts down; there were moments when we dared not catch each other's eyes." Then Mr Farmer came into the room, uncomfortable in a thick suit and a collar.

> Then, for the first time since heaven knows when, the double doors were flung open by our Hostess. She had discarded her apron, and stood in full bombazine welcoming us to the supper-table, as if she had not already met her guests at the front door. And what a supper-table!

Mrs Farmer had gone to great lengths. There was a ham, a great joint of beef, a raised pie and birds among dishes of butter and pickles and salads, sauce-boats of dressing and slabs of home-made bread. The sideboard groaned under fruit-tarts, trifles, cheesecakes and the flagons of rough cider. They all ate heartily, with Mrs Farmer pressing food on them from the top of the table, refilling their tankards with more cider and as the evening progressed and more cider was drunk, the conversation started to flow. "As tongues wagged and self-consciousness waned, Mr Farmer took off his collar.

'Father!' from his scandalized Better Half.

'Can't help it, Mother; I'm sweaty!' he beamed; and took off his coat."

For the rest of the meal, Mr Farmer sat in his shirt-sleeves. Mrs Farmer disapproved but her party was a great success, with her literary guests around her laughing and talking. After the cheese Mrs Farmer rose, as did Eleanor

Farjeon, Helen Thomas and Elinor Frost. Mr Farmer too rose from his chair, but the rest of the guests found it a little more difficult.

"The Poets attempted to rise, relapsed on to their seats, and regarded each other with comical consternation. They were perfectly sober, though exceedingly gay; but the gallons of strong cider, against which I had been inoculated, had gone to their legs and not one of them could stand without support. I saw Edward and Robert stagger to their feet, clutch each other, and go down; they rose again with great caution, clinging together. On the other side of the table Gibson and Abercrombie were behaving similarly. Two brace of poets staggered out into the moonlight and went hilariously homeward like two sets of Siamese Twins. I have boasted ever since of the night when I drank all the poets of Gloucestershire under the table."

NOTES

1 Eleanor Farjeon, *Edward Thomas: The Last Four Years*, (Oxford University Press, 1979). This source provides all the quotations in this chapter.

After Dymock

By the winter of 1914 the Dymock interlude was nearly over. The call to arms and war effort saw the poets disperse. Two, Brooke and Thomas, were to die in the war, both still young men and with so much potential still to realise. Frost returned to America in 1915 where he found that he had become quite famous in his absence, while Abercrombie and Gibson were to slip gradually into near oblivion. Drinkwater, in poetry at least, never achieved the wide acclaim of his fellows, though his work has always had its devotees and in recent years there has been something of a revival of interest: some of his poems have been set to music, along with those of Gurney, Haines and Harvey and recorded by the Gloucestershire based singer-songwriter Johnny Coppin.

At the end of August 1914, Edward Thomas's family returned to Petersfield while Thomas went on a trip to some of the major cities to research two articles for *The English Review* on what ordinary people were saying about the war. "I left Ledbury on Wednesday & Helen & the children went home" he wrote to Gordon Bottomley from Coventry on September 3rd, 1914. "I shall be glad to be back with them. I saw too little of Abercrombie, too much of Gibson & Frost daily – our families interwove all day long & we enjoyed many days but with all sorts of mixed feelings." Later that month he wrote again to Bottomley about the second issue of *New Numbers*, which he had yet to see:

> If Abercrombie's contribution is on the 'Massacre of Innocents' I don't think much of it. I saw it in proof. It seemed to me not much more than a hastily turning to the theme in an almost journalistic effort. Drinkwater must be hopeless in this incarnation & I haven't heard of another. Gibson I gather is likely to be just sending suitable things to the market he has discovered. But I don't see that Abercrombie can hurt him. Brooke was going to war when I last heard.

Thomas was soon to enlist, much to the surprise of many of his friends, even though he hated the prevalent jingoism. When Eleanor Farjeon asked him why he was fighting, Thomas bent down, picked up some soil and simply said "for this". It was at Leddington that Thomas realised he had to fight in the war, as he explained in his article 'This England'.

> It was the end of a wet day; at least, it had begun wet, had turned warm and muggy, and at last fine but still cloudy. The sky was banded with rough masses in the north-west, but the moon, a stout orange crescent, hung free of cloud near the horizon. At one stroke, I thought, like many other people, what things that

94

same new moon sees eastward about the Meuse in France. Of those who could not see it there, not blinded by smoke, pain or excitement, how many saw it and heeded? I was deluged, in a second stroke, by another thought, or something that overpowered thought. All I can tell is, it seemed to me that either I had never loved England, or I had loved it foolishly, aesthetically, like a slave, not having realized that it was not mine unless I were willing and prepared to die rather than leave it as Belgian women and old men and children had left their country. Something I had omitted. Something, I felt, had to be done before I could look again composedly at English landscape, at the elms and poplars about the houses, at the purple-headed wood-betony with two pairs of dark leaves on a stiff stem, who stood sentinel among the grasses or bracken by hedge-side or wood's-edge. What he stood sentinel for I did not know, any more than what I had got to do.[1]

Frost had suggested he join him in America where together they would run a farm. Frost hoped to set him free from journalism and thought that perhaps there he would find a market for what he so obviously wanted to do – write verse. Instead, Thomas joined the Artists' Rifles and in many respects it was this that set him free. He seemed to have found elusive inner peace and a freedom by receiving, for the first time, a regular income: no longer did he have to write in order to support his family.

Thomas's association with Gloucestershire did not end with the outbreak of the war. He continued to visit Frost and Haines and there were many occasions to continue their 'walks-talking' as Frost so aptly called them, and what Haines described in a local newspaper as:

> . . . enchanting walks over the Cotswolds and Dean Forest, both before he enlisted and after, and, indeed, up to a few days before he sailed for France; and ever the same exquisite talk on poetry and the poets, on his own verse often, or that of others oftener; on England and the English; on the birds and the flowers and the ordinary everyday people; on everything that was at once usual and beautiful, and therefore likely to be missed by anyone but a poet.[2]

He returned towards the end of 1914 to The Gallows where the Frosts were now staying for the winter. The clothes on the line in the garden at Ryton, "violently blowing in the wind and crackle like a rising woodfire"[3] were remembered in 'Up in the wind':

> . . . And the linen crackles on the line
> Like a woodfire rising . . .

In the following June, Thomas returned again, cycling there accompanied as far as Stroud by Jesse Berridge and staying for one night *en route* with Arthur Ransome. While in Ryton he cycled with John Haines to the top of May Hill, the massive hill overlooking the Leadon Valley and well within view of Oldfields and Little Iddens.

After Dymock

Again and again we saw, instead of solid things, dark or bright, never more than half a mile off, the complete broad dome of a high hill six miles distant, a beautiful hill itself, but especially seen thus, always unexpectedly, through gaps in this narrow country, as through a window. Moreover, we knew that from the summit, between a few old Scots firs and the young ones of the plantation, we could command the Severn and the Cotswolds on the one hand, and on the other the Wye, the Forest of Dean, the island hills of North Monmouthshire, dark and massive, the remote Black Mountains pale and cloud-like, far beyond them in Wales.

It was sitting up on top of May Hill, while Haines went off 'botanising', that Edward Thomas wrote the beautiful 'Words':

WORDS

Out of us all
That makes rhymes,
Will you choose
Sometimes –
As the winds use
A crack in a wall
Or a drain.
Their joy or their pain
To whistle through –
Choose me,
You English words?

I know you:
You are light as dreams,
Tough as oak,
Precious as gold,
As poppies and corn
Or an old cloak:
Sweet as our birds
To the ear,
As the burnet rose
In the heat
Of Midsummer:
Strange as the races
Of dead and unborn:
Strange and sweet
Equally,
And familiar,
To the eye,
As the dearest faces
That a man knows,
And as lost homes are:

But though older far
Than oldest yew, –
As our hills are, old, –
Worn new
Again and again,
Young as our streams
After rain:
And as dear
As the earth which you prove
That we love.

Make me content
With some sweetness
From Wales
Whose nightingales
Have no wings, –
From Wiltshire and Kent
And Herefordshire,
And the villages there, –
From the names, and the things
No less.
Let me sometimes dance
With you,
Or climb
Or stand perchance
In ecstasy,
Fixed and free
In a rhyme,
As poets do.

Years later Ivor Gurney recited this poem at a London literary dinner, saying that it stated all that need be said about the English language.

Thomas kept in touch with Abercrombie and Gibson and corresponded regularly with Frost. He dreamed of the time that he and the American had spent together at Leddington, writing to Frost on July 22nd, 1915: "A month or two I dreamt we were walking near Leddington but we lost one another in a strange place and I woke saying to myself 'Somehow, someday I shall be here again', which I made the last line of some verses". The verses were 'A Dream (Sonnet 1):

A DREAM (SONNET 1)

Over known fields with an old friend in dream
I walked, but came sudden to a strange stream.
Its dark waters were bursting out most bright
From a great mountain's heart into the light.

They ran a short course under the sun, then back
Into a pit they plunged, once more as black
As at their birth: and I stood thinking there
How white, had the day shone on them, they were,
Heaving and coiling. So by the roar and hiss
And by the mighty motion of the abyss
I was bemused, that I forgot my friend
And neither saw nor sought him till the end,
When I awoke from waters unto men
Saying: 'I shall be here some day again.'

Edward Thomas also received a poem from Robert Frost, written for him and sent to France:

THE ROAD NOT TAKEN

Two roads diverged in a yellow wood,
And sorry I could not travel both
And be one traveller, long I stood
And looked down one as far as I could
To where it bent in the undergrowth;

Then took the other, as just as fair,
And having perhaps the better claim,
Because it was grassy and wanted wear;
Though as for that passing there
Had worn them really about the same,

And both that morning equally lay
In leaves no step had trodden black.
Oh, I kept the first for another day!
Yet knowing how way leads on to way,
I doubted if I should ever come back.

I shall be telling this with a sigh
Somewhere ages and ages hence:
Two roads diverged in a wood, and I –
I took the one less travelled by,
And that has made all the difference.

Thomas's poem 'The Huxter', about a hunchbacked pedlar, also had its links with his stay at Leddington: in his Field Note Book 77 he recorded: "24, Aug. 1914: Ledbury – met a huckster."

He has a hump like an ape on his back;
He has of money a plentiful lack;
And but for a gay coat of double his girth
There is not a plainer thing on the earth
    This fine May morning.

But the huxter has a bottle of beer;
He drives a cart and his wife sits near
Who does not heed his lack or his hump;
And they laugh as down the lane they bump
   This fine May morning.

He had now begun to write poetry with all the zeal of someone who has discovered his direction after many years in a wilderness. His friends were quick to realise that here was a major poet and gave him as much help as was possible when the war was drastically restricting book publication let alone the poetry of an 'unknown' poet. Once again the Gloucestershire connection was invaluable. When Abercrombie and Robert Trevelyan visited Gordon Bottomley to discuss the compilation of *An Annual of New Poetry* they were shown a bundle of Thomas's work and agreed to include some in their planned anthology. Thomas instructed that they be published under the pseudonym Edward Eastaway, for he was not yet sure of his own merit as a poet and perhaps did not want to risk damaging his considerable reputation. These were the only poems he ever saw in print because on Monday April 9th, 1917 he died from the blast of a shell at Arras, not at Vimy Ridge where it was originally thought he had been killed and which became the accepted version for some years, as Frost wrote:

TO E.T.

I slumbered with your poems on my breast
Spread open as I dropped them, half-read through
Like dove wings on a figure on a tomb
To see, if in the dream they brought of you,

I might not have the chance I missed in life
Through some delay, and call you to your face
First soldier, and then poet, and then both,
Who died a soldier-poet of your race.

I meant, you meant, that nothing should remain
Unsaid between us, brother, and this remained —
And one thing more that was not then to say:
The Victory for what it lost and gained.

You went to meet the shell's embrace of fire
On Vimy Ridge; and when you fell that day
The war seemed over more for you than me,
But now for me than you — the other way.

How over, though, for even me who knew
The foe thrust back unsafe beyond the Rhine,
If I was not to speak of it to you
And see you pleased once more with words of mine?

Rupert Brooke enlisted in September 1914 as a sub-lieutenant in the Royal Naval Volunteer Reserves. By October, he was in France and in battle. His almost joyous attitude to joining the war effort and his seeming desire for a glorious death in battle made him a romantic hero and it was his writings that persuaded many young poets to join in this 'great adventure'. The news that poets were fighting – and dying – in the war did much to encourage others to join up. It was not that Brooke glorified war, however, but he did celebrate participating in it. He was acutely aware of its horror – many of his contemporaries from school days died in the early months – but he was equally conscious of the sacrifice that was being made by the French and the Belgians and felt that England would be shamed if it too did not contribute. "There shouldn't be war – but what's to be done but fight Prussia?" he wrote to Lowes Dickinson, a Cambridge friend.

A few months later he had joined 'A' Company of the Hood Battalion and was training at Blandford in Dorset, from where he wrote to John Drinkwater:

It was ignoble of me not to answer. But one becomes ignoble at this game. Or, at least, brutish. The mind becomes, not unpleasantly, submerged. The days go by. I plough through mud: march: drill: eat and sleep: and do not question more. There was some affair at Antwerp, I remember. I have a recollection of a burning city, the din of cannonades, a shattered railway-station, my sailors bivouacking in the grounds of a deserted château, refugees coming out of the darkness . . . But most of the time I was thinking of food, or marching straight, or what to say to the men, or, mostly, not thinking at all. It was rather exhilarating, or rather terrible. But I don't think one is very swift to sensations in these parts of life. Still, it's the only life for me, just now. The training is a bloody bore. But on service one has a great feeling of fellowship, and a fine thrill, like nothing else in the world. And I'd not be able to exist, for torment, if I weren't doing it. Not a bad place and time to die, Belgium, 1915? I want to kill my Prussian first. Better than coughing out a civilian soul amid bed-clothes and disinfectant and gulping medicines in 1950. The world'll be tame enough after the war, for those that see it. I had hopes that England'ld get on her legs again, achieve youth and merriment, and slough the things I loathe – capitalism and feminism and hermaphroditism and the rest. But on maturer consideration, pursued over muddy miles of Dorset, I think there'll not be much change. What there is for the better though. Certain sleepers have awoken in the heart.

Come and die. It'll be great fun. And there's great health in the preparation. The theatre's no place, now. If you stay there you'll not be able to start afresh with us when we come back. Peguy and Duhamel; and I don't know what others. I want to mix a few sacred and Apollonian English ashes with theirs, lest England be shamed. But first, or anyhow, borrow a car, pick up Wilfrid and Lascelles one Saturday, and come to Dorset; and on Saturday afternoon, or Sunday, or both, walk over the Roman downs with me, and drink greatly, and talk once more, and bury *New Numbers* with a *Resurgam*. I *may* have only four weeks more in England.

Rupert Brooke returned to Dymock just before leaving with the Hood Battalion as part of a landing force that was to take Constantinople. He stayed at The Gallows and Catherine Abercrombie remembered that he looked at the huge sloping field of scarlet poppies near their garden and said "I shall always remember that – always."[5] In a few weeks he was dead.

For Rupert Brooke, his 'corner of a foreign field' was the top of a hill on the Greek island of Skyros where he was buried after contracting acute septicaemia while on board a troop ship from a mosquito bite on his upper lip. He had never been very strong, especially following a serious illness in the South Seas, and he wasn't able to fight the blood poisoning. The lip began to swell and he began to complain of bad back and head pains. By Thursday April 22nd the doctors had diagnosed blood poisoning and he was transferred to a French hospital ship. Winston Churchill, First Lord of the Admiralty, was informed and telephoned Marsh with the news that Brooke's condition was grave. At 4.46 on April 23rd Brooke died, aged 27. After the war a statue, subscribed by English, French and Dutch admirers was erected to his memory on the island and Abercrombie was invited to travel to Skyros to give the English oration at the dedication ceremony. Abercrombie also remembered Rupert Brooke in a more personal way – in verse:

R.B.

Beautiful life! As air delights to find
   The white heat of a fire and to be flame,
The eager world throng'd into his glowing mind
   And flame of burning beauty there became.

All things were turned to fire in him, and cast
   The light of their transfiguring round his ways.
His secret gleamed upon us; where he past
   He shone; he brought with him a golden place.

It was the purest fire of life that shone,
   This angel brightness visiting our mould.
Life knew no way to make life lovelier, none;
   But then came Death: 'I know the way.
Behold!'

Gibson, who had drawn so much inspiration from his time in Dymock, showed his feelings of comradeship with Abercrombie, Frost and Brooke in verse. To Abercrombie he dedicated 'Trees', alluding in it to evenings spent in the garden of The Gallows, reading poetry by the light of the campfire under the great elms in that halcyon summer before the war engulfed them:

TREES
(To Lascelles Abercrombie)

The flames half lit the cavernous mystery
Of the over-arching elm that loomed profound
And mountainous above us, from the ground
Soaring to midnight stars majestically,
As, under the shelter of that ageless tree
In a rapt dreaming circle we lay around
The crackling faggots, listening to the sound
Of old words moving in new harmony.

And as you read before our wondering eyes
Arose another tree of mighty girth,
Crested with stars though rooted to the earth,
Its heavy-foliaged branches lit with gleams
Of ruddy firelight and the light of dreams,
Soaring immortal to eternal skies.

'Trees' was first published in the small collection of Gibson's verse, *Friends*, published in 1916, which he dedicated to the memory of Rupert Brooke. It included the simple, moving 'To the Memory of Rupert Brooke' and the longer 'Rupert Brooke' in which he remembered how the young poet had gazed at the poppies in the field near The Gallows and his own visit to stay at The Old Vicarage, Grantchester.

TO THE MEMORY OF RUPERT BROOKE
23rd April 1915

He's gone.
I do not understand:
I only know
That as he turned to go
And waved his hand
In his young eyes a sudden glory shone,
And I was dazzled by a sunset glow,
And he was gone.

RUPERT BROOKE

I

Your face was lifted to the golden sky
Ablaze beyond the black roofs of the square
As flame on flame leapt, flourishing in air
Its tumult of red stars exultantly
To the cold constellations dim and high;

And, as we neared, the roaring ruddy flare
Kindled to gold your throat and brow and hair
Until you burned, a flame of ecstasy.

The golden head goes down into the night
Quenched in cold gloom – and yet again you stand
Beside me now with lifted face alight
As, flame to flame and fire to fire, you burn . . .
Then, recollecting, laughingly you turn
And look into my eyes and take my hand.

II

Once in my garret – you being far away
Tramping the hills and breathing upland air
Or so I fancied – brooding in my chair,
I watched the London sunlight feeble and grey
Dapple my desk, too tired to labour more,
When, looking up, I saw you standing there,
Although I'd caught no footstep on the stair
Like sudden April at my open door.

Though now beyond earth's farthest hills you fare,
Song-crowned, immortal, sometimes it seems to me
That if I listen very quietly
Perhaps I'll hear your footstep on the stair
And see you, standing with your angel air,
Fresh from the uplands of eternity.

III

Your eyes rejoiced in colour's ecstasy,
Fulfilling even their uttermost desire,
When, over a great sunlit field afire
With windy poppies streaming like a sea
Of scarlet flame that flaunted riotously
Among green orchards of that western shire,
You gazed as though your heart could never tire
Of life's red flood in summer revelry.

And as I watched you, little thought had I
How soon beneath the dim, low-drifting sky
Your soul should wander down the darkling way
With eyes that peer a little wistfully,
Half-glad, half-sad, remembering, as they see
Lethean poppies shrivelling ashen grey.

IV

October chestnuts showered their perishing gold
Over us as beside the stream we lay

After Dymock

In the old vicarage garden that blue day,
Talking of verse and all the manifold
Delights a little net of words may hold,
While in the sunlight water-voles at play
Dived under a trailing crimson bramble spray,
And walnuts thudded on the soft black mould.

Your soul goes down unto a darker stream
Alone, O friend, yet even in death's deep night
Your eyes may grow accustomed to the dark,
And Styx for you may have the ripple and gleam
Of your familiar river, and Charon's bark
Tarry by that old garden of your delight.

In the first part of this poem, Gibson remembered how he had first met Brooke with Marsh the night the three of them had gone to see a huge blaze in a London timber yard in September 1912, the week that the idea of compiling the anthology of Georgian Poetry had been born. It is a memory that recurs in another verse by Gibson: 'To Edward Marsh (In Memory of Rupert Brooke)' written in June 1915:

TO EDWARD MARSH
(IN MEMORY OF RUPERT BROOKE)

The night we saw the stacks of timber blaze
To terrible golden fury, young and strong
He watched between us with dream-dazzled gaze
Aflame and burning like a god of song,
As we together stood against the throng
Drawn from the midnight of the city ways.

To-night the world about us is ablaze
And he is dead, is dead . . . Yet, young and strong,
He watches with us still with deathless gaze
Aflame and burning like a god of song
As we together stand against the throng
Drawn from the bottomless midnight of hell's ways.

Rupert Brooke bequeathed to both Abercrombie and Gibson a handsome gift, and one that was to grow in value as the Brooke legend attracted a fame beyond that of his poetry. Sir Edward Marsh was naturally designated by Brooke to be his literary executor, but it was Gibson, Abercrombie and Walter de la Mare who became heirs to his royalties. He also named them as his heirs in a letter to his mother, in which he asked that the capital of his allowance from her be distributed amongst them and that on her death she left them some of the money she would have left him: "If I can set them free, to any extent, to write the poetry and plays and books they want to, my death will bring more gain than loss." After settling his debts, Mrs Brooke paid to each of his heirs the sum of £166. 19s.8d, the first instalment to them of his inheritance – a gift that was to amount considerably; up to 1932, 37 impressions of Brooke's poems were printed, totalling nearly 100,000 copies.

In July 1915, after visiting Brooke's mother in Rugby, Marsh travelled to Gloucestershire and stayed with the Gibsons at their old cottage where he was given the attic room away from the household noises. For eight days he worked on a memoir of his friend, each evening reading to his hosts what he had written that day. At 2 a.m. on July 27th he finished it, although because of problems with Mrs Brooke it was not published until many years later. By then it had become a distressing nightmare rather than the intended labour of love in memory of a dear friend.

Gibson made several attempts to enlist, but was turned down because of his poor eyesight. In 1917, however, after returning from a lecture tour of the United States, he was accepted by the Army Service Corps, and served for two years. He was fortunate in having to spend only a few months at the Front. His war poetry was extremely graphic with none of the heroicism of Brooke but a typical down-to-earth quality, such as betting food in the trenches, while the shells screeched overhead, whether Hull United would beat Halifax ('Breakfast') and the man 'In the Ambulance' singing, despite having lost both legs:

> Two rows of cabbages
> Two of curly-greens
> Two rows of early peas
> Two of kidney-beans

From the hell of the trenches, Gibson remembered the tranquillity of Dymock in the springtime, with its fields of daffodils, its orchards and its lambs:

> I sit beside the brazier's glow,
> And, drowsing in the heat,
> I dream of daffodils that blow,
> And lambs that frisk and bleat –
>
> Black lambs that frolic in the snow
> Among the daffodils,
> In a far orchard that I know
> Beneath the Malvern hills.
>
> Next year the daffodils will blow
> And lambs will frisk and bleat;
> But I'll not feel the brazier's glow,
> Nor any cold or heat.

In a different mood, Gibson wrote:

> Last year I was hoeing,
> Hoeing mangel-wurzels,
> Hoeing mangel-wurzels all day in the sun,
> Hoeing for the squire,
> Down in Gloucestershire,
> Willy-nilly till the sweaty job was done.
>
> Now I'm in the 'wurzels,
> In the mangel-wurzels,
> All day in the 'wurzels 'neath the Belgian sun.
> But among this little lot
> It's a different job I've got –
> For you don't hoe mangel-wurzels with a gun.

The simplicity of these service poems is also found in two poems published in 1917 in *Whin*: 'Stow-on-the-Wold', about a countryman who lost six sons in the fighting, and 'Bourton-on-the-Water' in which the soldier, surrounded by the sounds of slaughter, remembers how he and his "dear" had walked through the Cotswold town the previous year. A third poem, 'Northleach', is about the Gloucester prison and was probably written after a conversation with a fellow soldier.

STOW-ON-THE-WOLD

> I met an old man at Stow-on-the-Wold,
> Who shook and shivered as though with cold.
>
> And he said to me: "Six sons I had,
> And each was a tall and a lively lad.
>
> "But all of them went to France with the guns,
> They went together, my six tall sons.
>
> "Six sons I had, six sons I had —
> And each was a tall and a lively lad."

BOURTON-ON-THE-WATER

> The Windrush ripples cool and clear
> Through Bourton-on-the-Water;
> And I was walking with my dear
> Through Bourton-on-the-Water,
> This very day last year.
>
> And now above the guns I hear,
> Above the sounds of slaughter,

While I am thinking of my dear,
I hear above the slaughter,
The voice I heard last year.

The Windrush rippling cool and clear
Through Bourton-on-the-Water,
When I was walking with my dear
Through Bourton-on-the-Water,
This very day last year.

NORTHLEACH

As I came out of Northleach Gaol,
To see the world outside,
There came a sudden blast of hail,
And the wind blew cold across the wold,
And the world seemed far too wide.

O take me back to Northleach Gaol,
'Tis there I would abide,
Secure from snow and rain and hail,
And the wind so cold across the wold,
Secure and snug inside.

Some months after the outbreak of the war Gibson, in uniform, chanced to meet John Haines on Paddington Station, but it was not a happy reunion. Gibson's wife, who had recently given birth, had fallen down the stairs of The Old Nail Shop and been seriously hurt. She had been rushed to Malvern hospital and Gibson had been given leave to visit her but was having problems because of the late hour and army 'red tape': "He was in a dreadful state of mind, and he was forced to go round by Worcester, because the regulations bade him, and there was no train, and he could not travel down to Gloucester with me, his friend, though I would somehow have got him out there that night or early next morning."[6]

Gibson continued to write after the war and a volume of his collected poems was published in 1926. His last book, *Within Four Walls*, was published in 1950, the year his wife Geraldine died. Gibson never again achieved the level of success of his Dymock days, though his poems still appear occasionally in anthologies. With the help of Brooke's legacy he managed to live quite comfortably on his writing and when he died, in Weybridge, Surrey in 1962, he left £10,000 – a considerable sum for those days, especially for a poet.

Drinkwater spent the war in the theatre, and made his mark on the history of the English stage, taking plays not just to the West End but to America and

Paris as well. He continued to write poetry, too, including the fine though little known 'Nineteen-Fifteen':

NINETEEN-FIFTEEN

On a ploughland hill against the sky,
Over the barley, over the rye,
Time, which is now a black pine tree,
Holds out his arms and mocks at me –

'In the year of your Lord Nineteen-fifteen
The acres are ploughed and the acres are green,
And the calves and the lambs and the foals are born,
But man the angel is all forlorn.

'The cropping cattle, the swallow's wing,
The wagon team and the pasture spring,
Move in their seasons and are most wise,
But man, whose image is in the skies,

'Who is master of all, whose hand achieves
The church and the barn and the homestead eaves –
How are the works of his wisdom seen
In the year of your Lord Nineteen-fifteen?'

A regular visitor to Dymock and Gloucestershire before the war, Drinkwater came to live in the county as the conflict came to an end. In 1916, with Joseph Southall and Arthur Gaskin, he visited the artist, William Rothenstein, at Iles Farm in Far Oakridge, a small village overlooking The Golden Valley near Stroud. Rothenstein had purchased the run-down 17th century farmhouse, set in 55 acres, four years earlier and restored it. His home had become a centre for writers and artists in much the same way as Dymock had. Drinkwater fell in love with the area where Cotswold cottages sat in tiny hamlets and small villages on the hills led down to the canal and the River Frome. When the furnished Winston's Cottage became available he rented it and became a neighbour of the famous artist. In his *Cotswold Characters*, in which he so lovingly described some of his less eminent but nevertheless colourful neighbours, Drinkwater wrote of the countryside of his newly adopted home as "the most beautiful in England" and of his new home "I am myself the tenant of a small cottage on a byway that is passed by a stranger hardly once a week."[7]

Drinkwater had not been the first famous occupant of the small cottage; Rothenstein's close friend Max Beerbohm spent most of the war years here. Beerbohm, who produced his classic collection *Rossetti and his Circle* at

Winston's Cottage, made few concessions to country living, going for walks as if dressed for the West End, in spats, trilby, kid leather gloves and carrying a silver topped cane. Drinkwater, on the other hand, relished country living, coming out each morning dressed in shorts and a blue shirt with open collar to fetch drinking water from the nearby spring and delighting to walk the lanes and talk to the local people. Their very different views of rural life at Oakridge is clearly illustrated in two poems; the first, 'Cottage Song' is by Drinkwater and his love of his new home is clearly to be seen while the second, titled 'Same Cottage – but Another Song, of Another Season' shows a contrasting side to life at Winston's Cottage, written with all Beerbohm's wit and, he admitted in a postscript, "a wicked echo of so lovely a poem".

COTTAGE SONG

Morning and night I bring
Clear water from the spring,
And through the lyric noon
I hear the larks in tune,
And when the shadows fall
There's providence for all.

My garden is alight
With currants red and white;
And my blue curtains peep
On starry courses deep,
When down her silver tides
The moon on Cotswold rides.

My path of paven grey
In thoroughfare all day
For fellowship, till time
Bids us with candles, climb
The little whitewashed stair
Above my lavender.

SAME COTTAGE – BUT ANOTHER SONG, OF ANOTHER SEASON

Morning and night I found
White snow upon the ground,
And on the tragic well
Grey ice had cast her spell.
A dearth of wood and coal
Lay heavy on my soul.

My garden was a scene
Of weeds and nettles green,
My window-panes had holes
Through which, all night, lost souls
Peered from the desert road,
And starved cocks faintly crowed.

My path of cinders black
Had an abundant lack
Of visitors, till time
Bade us with boxes climb
The train that hurries on
To old warm Paddington.

Rothenstein's Iles Farm was also described in verse by John Drinkwater:

Here is a theme for graver tones
Than now I sing.
It shelters you; it is a pole
For thought upon your travelling;
Here dreams established are in stones,
To mark and bring
Irresolutions to control
From truant wing.

But not of these my argument.
I celebrate,
Your hearth, your comfortable speech
Of young years and late,
Your courtesies that are content
To sow and wait,
For these as planets are to teach
My travel to your gate.

Rothenstein described Drinkwater in his memoirs as ". . . the poet incarnate, generous, high-minded, enthusiastic over the work of other poets, delighting in the countryside, in his little garden, in playing host to friends in his cottage."[8] He described how his children 'adored' the poet who used to play cricket and go fishing with them.

At the time, Drinkwater and his wife Kathleen were struggling financially and life at Far Oakridge was lived quite frugally. It was however an extremely productive period when Drinkwater completed his play *Abraham Lincoln* at Winston's Cottage, as Rothenstein recalled: "On the day he finished *Lincoln* he came bounding out of the cottage, met the children, and danced round with them, shouting 'I've finished my play! I've finished my play!" The play was to become a tremendous success, in America especially, and put the Drinkwaters' life on a firm financial position at last, but their marriage had begun to break up by the time they left Far Oakridge and Gloucestershire in 1921. Three years later they were divorced. Drinkwater later remarried, his second wife being the noted violinist Daisy Kennedy, daughter of an Australian schoolmaster and the former wife of the Russian pianist Besso Moiseiwitsch. Drinkwater died in 1937, only 55 years old. He had been seemingly tireless, putting great energy into everything he did, whether it was writing poetry, writing for the stage, acting or running the Birmingham theatre.

Abercrombie tried unsuccessfully to join up, failing every time on medical grounds. He volunteered instead to do steel-testing in a munitions factory leaving his beloved thatched house at Ryton in 1916 for Liverpool, where he was later joined by his family. Unlike many of his contemporaries and many younger writers who were inspired to write some of their best work during the war years, Abercrombie almost gave up writing. The engineer's shop seems to have killed the muse for the poet considered by many critics and fellow poets as one of the most talented of his era. Bottomley wrote to Edward Thomas on March 28th, 1917:

> I don't wonder at Abercrombie feeling as he does; it [presumably the loss of the desire to write] would be one of the few things that I should find definitely unendurable. When he was rejected for the Army, his great desire was to take some other kind of adventurous service, and for a long time he had a definite intention of joining George Trevelyan in Italy and working in a mountain ambulance. But all the time there was the cruel and uncertain threat of disease hanging over his wife, and I suppose he felt he couldn't go until he knew that she was safe . . . The weary round of ugliness and repetition in an engineer's shop or any kind of works or office is worse to bear than anything else for someone with such creative energy and vision as his and (at a guess) I fancy he felt it a hateful and hope-destroying slavery.

Abercrombie never fully returned to writing verse, which he later called his 'unrealised ambition', nor to living in Gloucestershire:

> "The finest curse you can put on a man is to wish him an ambition which he cannot attain – or, even better, which he can only attain to lose it again irrevocably. Mine was an ambition that would have harmed no one: it was but to live in the country and write poetry. I was not equal to it. Is fortune to blame for that? Only in the sense that I am what I am."[9]

He turned instead to writing prose and teaching. In 1919 he became lecturer in poetry at Liverpool University, later Professor of English Literature at Leeds University (1922–9) and at Bedford College, London (1929–35). In 1935 he became a Fellow of Merton College, Oxford. He was also in demand as a visiting lecturer, at amongst others, Trinity College, Cambridge; Bangor; Queen's University, Belfast; and Johns Hopkins University in Baltimore, USA. He also received honorary degrees from the University of Cambridge, Liverpool, Oxford, Manchester and Belfast and was elected Fellow of the British Academy in 1937, the year before he died in London on October 27th, 1938.

Although neither Abercrombie nor Gibson returned after the war to resume their pastoral life, they did make regular visits to the area and corresponded with some of the village people they had befriended, including Mrs Hyett of Gallows Cottage and Mrs Smyth of Greenway Cottage. Abercrombie gave lectures throughout the county. John Haines wrote of his skill as a lecturer: ". . . anyone who has ever heard him will remember the charm of his reading voice, the best reading voice of any poet known to me, or indeed of any man; every line was a thrill, and yet never a rhetorical touch or tone or gesture disturbed the listener's sense of perfection; this with anyone's poems, but to those privileged to hear him read his own the thrill was more exquisite still."[10] He was also a regular speaker at the Malvern Festival, held every August.

One of the 'bit part' players in the story, W.H. Davies, moved to Gloucestershire in 1930 to settle in Nailsworth, the former woollen mill town south of Stroud, where he lived until his death in 1940. His wandering spirit, which had sent him tramping across the United States decades before, seems not to have diminished, except in scale: in his 10 years in Nailsworth he moved no fewer than four times and never very far within the small town, the last being in the Watledge area behind Egypt Mill to a house called Glendower. John Haines remained the country solicitor in the city of Gloucester, where F.W. Harvey was to join him after the war in which the young Gloucestershire poet had spent many years in a prisoner-of-war camp. Haines wrote a series of reminiscences for a Gloucestershire weekly newspaper and eventually a slim volume of poems, mostly inspired by the county:

THE HIGH-ROAD

The little roads are quaint roads
    That wander where they will,
They wind their arms round all the farms
    And flirt with every hill,
But the high-road is my road
    And goes where I would go,
Its way it wends as man intends,
    For it was fashioned so.

After Dymock

The little roads are shy roads
  And care not to be seen,
'Twixt hedges hid they wind amid
  A labyrinth of green,
But the high-roads are bold roads
  And stare one in the face,
With banners white in all men's sight
  The land they proudly pace.

The little roads are faint roads
  And fear to walk alone,
They like the looks of friendly brooks
  And cots of country stone,
But the high-roads are proud roads
  And lord it like the King,
They stride the dale the hills to scale,
O'er wasting rivers they prevail,
  Nor yield to anything.

To all the little roads I know
  Delightful haunts belong –
In hidden state lurks Stanway gate
  The Stanway woods among,
The river walk between the Colnes
  From Fosseway lies apart,
While Slaughter seems amid its streams
To dwell in willow-pattern dreams
  Dreamt by a childish heart.

But give me on an autumn day
  That lordly road to trace
From Charlton Hill to Baunton Mill
  And Ciceter market place,
Or back, the way the Romans came
  Above a folded world
To Birdlip steep, where in a leap
The road doth to that valley sweep
  Where Severn lies unfurled.

The little roads are warm roads
  And fine to house within;
They grow great trees, escape the breeze
  And nurse the homely inn;
The high-roads are dry roads
  For many a thirsty mile,
But their wind and rain I will face again
  As I have done many a while.

Robert Frost returned to Dymock twice, in 1928 and 1957. The 1928 visit was one that had been in his mind for some time; three years earlier he had written to John Haines:

"Why don't I buy a ticket and hoist sail for England when I long to see you as much as I do! We would have to talk and walk in Leddington and Ryton if I came over. I should probably die of internal weeping . . . I can't tell you how homesick I am."

In August 1928, with his wife and daughter Marjorie, he set sail for Europe, stopping in France where Marjorie was to stay with a French family in Sèvres for six weeks while her parents were in England. Frost managed to spend some time with Haines at his home in Hucclecote, near Gloucester and one day the solicitor drove the Frosts to Dymock and to Little Iddens where the occupants of his old cottage showed them around. They also went to Ryton where The Gallows was becoming quite dilapidated.

During this stay in the county, Frost and Haines walked the hills of the Cotswolds and Churchdown Hill and once again they climbed May Hill, an emotional experience as uppermost in their minds, reports Haines, was the memory of Edward Thomas who had accompanied them so often to the top of the hill that dominated this part of Gloucestershire. From England, Frost travelled to Ireland, where he met Yeats, AE (George William Russell) and Padraic Colum, and then it was to London, staying at The Imperial Hotel in Russell Square, for a reading at Monro's Poetry Bookshop and meetings with Gibson and Abercrombie. The visit ended in late November when they sailed for France to pick up their daughter and return to the States.

Frost's 1957 visit had been arranged so he could receive honorary degrees from no fewer than four universities – Oxford, Cambridge, Durham and Dublin. While staying in London, Frost had originally planned to get in touch with Gibson, then living in Surrey. An American friend had visited Gibson three years earlier and had reported to Frost that the poet's memory was 'fleeting'; now he learnt that Gibson's memory had deteriorated even further and that he remembered practically nothing, so Frost thought better of a meeting.

Accompanied by his grand-daughter Lesley Francis, his biographer Lawrence Thompson and two representatives of *Time-Life* magazine, Beatrice Dobell and photographer Howard J. Sochurek, the octagenarian stayed the night of June 5th at the Greenway Hotel at Shurdington, between Cheltenham and Gloucester, where he was visited by his old friend John Haines. His first step the next day was to visit Gibson's old cottage where he was shown around by the occupant, Miss Gwendoline Dyer. The party then travelled to Little

Iddens, stopping opposite Mirables where Frost talked with Harry Blandford, who had been his neighbour all those years ago, and walked into a field so he could see his old house across the shallow valley as he had done on so many walks with Edward Thomas.

Frost seemed reluctant to enter the black and white timber framed cottage where he and his family had spent the summer of 1914, simply saying he remembered the box hedge and talking about the strawberries and cherries growing there.

The group then went on to Oldfields, but Frost did not go in. Last stop on the itinerary was the ruins of The Gallows, its courtyard filled with brambles and rubble and only part of the building, covered in ivy and undergrowth, still standing.

It was a strange and emotional day for the American, reliving memories of that glorious summer 43 years before when he and his close friend Thomas had walked the countryside, played with their children in the fields and orchards, talked ceaselessly of poetry under the old black beams of Little Iddens and visited their literary friends at Greenway Cross and Ryton.

Dymock had been a short interlude in the history of English poetry, but the impact of this 'poets' holiday' was out of all proportion to its brevity. The village once famous for its wild flowers and its fruit, is now known all over the world for the inspiration it gave to a group of poets living under the shadow of the First World War.

> "I have lived in Gloucestershire, and I have known what it is to have Wilfrid Gibson and Robert Frost as my neighbours; and John Drinkwater, Rupert Brooke, Edward Thomas, Will Davies, Bob Trevelyan, Arthur Ransome, have drunk my cider and talked in my garden. I make no cider now, and I have no garden. But once I lived in Gloucestershire."
>
> Lascelles Abercrombie, 1932[11]

NOTES

1   Edward Thomas, 'This England', *The Nation*, November 7th, 1914.
2   John Haines, *Gloucester Journal*, February 9th, 1935.
3   Recorded in Thomas's Field Note Books.
4   Edward Thomas, ibid.
5   Catherine Abercrombie, 'Memoirs of a Poet's Wife', *The Listener*, November 15th, 1956.
6   John Haines, *Gloucester Journal*, December 15th, 1934.
7   John Drinkwater, *Cotswold Characters*, (Oxford University Press, (Humphrey Milford), 1921).
8   William Rothenstein, *Men and Memories: Recollections 1872–1938*, (Chatto & Windus, 1978).
9   John Gawsworth, *Ten Contemporaries: Notes Towards Their Definitive Biography*, (Ernest Benn, 1932).
10 John Haines, 'Professor Lascelles Abercrombie: a Gloucestershire Poet', *Gloucester Journal*, January 12th, 1935.
11 John Gawsworth, ibid.

Bibliography

The following books and articles were the main printed sources used in the researching of this book. The author acknowledges the publishers' assistance in granting permission to quote from these works.

Abercrombie, Catherine, 'Memoirs of a Poet's Wife', *The Listener*, November 15th, 1956.

Abercrombie, Lascelles, *The Poems of Lascelles Abercrombie* (Oxford University Press (Humphrey Milford) 1930).

Brooke, Rupert, *The Collected Poems: With a memoir by Edward Marsh* (Sidgwick & Jackson, 1928).

Drinkwater, John, *Selected Poems* (Sidgwick & Jackson, 1922).

Drinkwater, John, *Cotswold Characters* (Oxford University Press, 1921).

Farjeon, Eleanor, *Edward Thomas: The Last Four Years* (Oxford University Press, 1979. Originally published as *Memoirs. Book 1: Edward Thomas, the Last Four Years*, OUP 1958).

Frost, Robert, *Collected Poems* (Jonathan Cape, 1951).

Frost, Robert, *Collected Poems* (Oxford University Press, 1951).

Gawsworth, John, *Ten Contemporaries: Notes towards their definitive biography* (Ernest Benn, 1932). Contained autobiographical essays by Lascelles Abercrombie and Wilfrid Gibson.

Gethyn-Jones, Rev. J.E., *Dymock Down the Ages* (privately printed, 1951; new edition, Alan Sutton, 1985).

Gethyn-Jones, Rev. J.E., *The Dymock School of Sculpture* (Phillimore & Co. 1979).

Gibson, Wilfrid W., *Collected Poems 1905–1925* (Macmillan, 1926).

Haines, John, 'Professor Lascelles Abercrombie: a Gloucestershire Poet', *Gloucester Journal*, January 12th, 1935.

Haines, John, 'Mr Robert Frost: an American Poet in Gloucestershire', *Gloucester Journal*, February 2nd, 1935.

Haines, John, 'Wilfrid Gibson', *Gloucester Journal*, December 15th, 1934.

Hassall, Christopher, *Rupert Brooke: a biography* (Faber & Faber, 1964).

Hassall, Christopher, *Edward Marsh: Patron of the Arts* (Longman, 1959).

Marsh, Jan, *Edward Thomas: a Poet for his Country* (Paul Elek, 1978).

Mertins, Louis, *Robert Frost: Life and Talks-Walking* (University of Oklahoma Press, 1965).

Moore, John, *The Life and Letters of Edward Thomas* (Heinemann, 1939; new edition, Alan Sutton, 1983).

Thomas, Edward, *Collected Poems: with a foreword by Walter de la Mare* (Faber & Faber 1936, new edition 1979).

Thomas, Edward, *In Pursuit of Spring* (Thomas Nelson, 1944; new edition Wildwood House, 1981).

Thomas, Edward, 'This England', *The Nation*, November 7th, 1914. This article was reprinted in *The Sheaf* (Cape, 1928) and more recently in *A Language Not to Be Betrayed: Selected Prose of Edward Thomas*, Carcanet Press, 1981.

Thomas, Helen, *As It Was* (Heinemann, 1926).

Thomas, Helen, *Time & Again: Memoirs & Letters* (Carcanet, 1978).

Thomas, Helen, *World Without End* (Heinemann, 1931).

As It Was and *World Without End* were published together by Heinemann in 1935 and by Faber & Faber in 1956 and 1972. They were more recently published together, with a selection from *Time & Again* and a section from Myfanwy Thomas' memoir *One of these Fine Days* (originally Carcanet, 1982), in one volume called *Under Storm's Wing* (Carcanet, 1988).

Thomas, R. George (ed), *The Collected Poems of Edward Thomas* (Oxford University Press, 1978; new edition 1981 & 1987).

Thomas, R. George (ed), *Letters from Edward Thomas to Gordon Bottomley* (Oxford University Press, 1968).

Thompson, Lawrence, *Robert Frost: The Early Years 1894-1915* (Holt, Rinehart & Winston, 1966 (USA)).

Thompson, Lawrence, *Selected Letters of Robert Frost* (Cape, 1965).

Townsend, Frances, *The Laureate of Gloucestershire. The Life and Work of F.W. Harvey, 1888-1957* (Redcliffe Press Ltd, 1988).

Zytaruk, G. & Boulton, J.T. (eds), *The Letters of D.H. Lawrence, Volume II June 1913 - October 1916* (Cambridge University Press, 1981).

List of Illustrations

between pages 64 and 65

List of poems

The following poems are mentioned in the text. Those in italic are reproduced in full.

Index

Index